Weekend Warriors

Men of Professional Lacrosse

Jack McDermott

New Chapter Press

Published by New Chapter Press
ISBN 0-94225-738-3
Printed in the United States of America

Special thanks to Wendy Lestina for writing and editing assistance
Cover and interior design: Visible Logic
Cover photo: Ryan Boyle by Ron Stenn
Interior photo credits:
Dan Ladouceur – Abelimages
Regy Thorpe – 20 Toe Photo
Ryan McNish – Courtesy of Calgary Roughnecks
Richard Morgan – Jeff Hinds
Gavin Prout – Michael Martin Photography
Kasey Beirnes – Bruce Kluckhohn
Del Halladay – Elephant Island Orchard Wines
Bruce Murray – Courtesy of Arizona Sting
Kyle Sweeney – Courtesy of Kyle Sweeney
Armando Polanco – Henny Abrams
Marshall Abrams – 20 Toe Photo
Ryan Boyle – Henny Abrams
Brian Langtry – Michael Martin Photography
Chris McKay – Courtesy of Arizona Sting
Pat Jones – Courtesy of Pat Jones

Acknowledgements

As with any writing project, there are numerous individuals who were vital to the completion of this book. First and foremost are the players themselves. Unlike the NFL, NBA and Major League Baseball players, the 15 players featured in this book do not have an "off season" to relax and play golf. To the contrary, they have families, full-time jobs, commitments on a year-round basis, and thus graciously sacrificed their own free time (usually at night or on weekends) to be interviewed for this project.

A special thanks goes to Wayne Lafluer for acting as a consultant on the project and giving initial feedback on rough drafts, not to mention arranging the interview with Marshall Abrams. The project received generous help from several PR directors of National Lacrosse League franchises who not only suggested players that fit into the theme of our project, but who also encouraged the players to find time to be interviewed. In no particular order, the assistance of Emily Corcoran of the Portland Lumberjax, Rob Crean of the Buffalo Bandits, Rick Bowness Jr. of the Arizona Sting, Mitch Redshaw of the Calgary Roughnecks, Dan Rowland of the Colorado Mammoth, Craig Rybczynski of the Rochester Knighthawks and Andy Watson of the Toronto Rock were all indispensable for the completion of this book.

I would also like to thank Jeff Tierney, Director of Public Relations of the NLL, who forwarded several articles, and had several good ideas to get the project underway. I also enjoyed the recollections of Union College's head lacrosse coach (formerly head coach at Herkimer Community College), Paul Wehrum, who shared his memories of Regy Thorpe (of the NLL's Rochester Knighthawks, and the MLL's Rochester Rattlers). I would also like to thank Isabelle Hodge, of the WTA tour—not just for arranging interviews with Gavin Prout—but also for sharing information about the world tennis tour as a contrast to the more modest lifestyles of professional lacrosse players.

There were several individuals who were co-workers of professional lacrosse players, and agreed to share their observations of how these players interact in a more traditional work environment. A list of these people includes: Karen Palmer (Regy Thorpe), Matt Tucker (Kasey Beirnes), Doug Weddell (Del Halladay), Todd Ballard (Bruce Murray), Wally Wilson (Pat Jones & Dan Ladouceur), Stephanie Ruyle (Armando Polanco), Rob Lindsey (Ryan Boyle), and Wayne Lafluer (Marshall Abrams & Regy Thorpe).

And finally a special thanks to Angela Batinovich, the owner/president of the Portland Lumberjax who was interviewed not just about the three Lumberjax players who appear in this book, but also about her thoughts on the growth and success of the National Lacrosse League as well. Regrettably not all of her observations made it into the final draft, but her help was important in shaping the introduction to this book.

—Jack McDermott

Table of Contents

Introduction

Mr. Langtry teaches humanities and literature to seventh and eighth graders at the Challenge School in the Cheery Creek School District near Denver, Colo. Mr. Langtry, who has a master's degree in teaching, guides his students through lessons on the Middle East, China, the Russian revolution, and literature; he instructs though literature, bringing into the study of Russian history, using such works as *Animal Farm*.

"I like teaching the Orwell books," Mr. Langtry says. "I encourage the kids to identify from the real people in the history of the Communist revolution, the characters in the book."

But sometimes, Mr. Langtry comes to class with a black eye.

Because when he's not teaching, Mr. Langtry is Brian Langtry, a "Weekend Warrior," a full-season professional lacrosse player who is a forward for both the Colorado Mammoth of the National Lacrosse League (NLL: the indoor, January-to-May game), and the Denver Outlaws of Major League Lacrosse (MLL, the May-August outdoor game).

In having two jobs, in being a hero both on and off the field, Brian Langtry is not unique—his sport is. Unlike the four major pro sports—football, baseball, basketball and hockey—lacrosse players cannot support themselves and their families through the earnings of the game alone. Rookie league salaries average $6,000 a year; high-end league salaries are slightly over $20,000. The result? During the week, professional lacrosse players are students, coaches, businessmen, service technicians, computer specialists, construction workers, policemen, financial analysts, insurance executives, firefighters, and, as is Brian Langtry, teachers. In vivid contrast to the glamorous, media-hyped stars of other professional sports, these men are "ordinary" people with "ordinary" jobs who just happen to have extraordinary abilities on the lacrosse field.

The players' salaries, very low relative to those in other professional sports, have had a direct effect on creating a family-friendly athletic event: in most lacrosse arenas—a single adult admission is $10; some offer $5 tickets. While the cheap price of curiosity may draw lacrosse first-timers to a game, the game itself—with the checking, hitting, quick-line changes, and fighting of hockey; the screens, picks man—and zone-defenses of basketball; the stick-handling technical skills of tennis and baseball; and the up-and-down action and passing of soccer—quickly hooks a new spectator. Also, in the twenty-one-year-old National Lacrosse League, games average 25 goals a game—a 13–12 final score is typical—which translates into continual excitement and celebration, a big plus with fans. In 2006, NLL games, for the first time, drew over one million spectators, prompting Reebok to invest over $10 million with the league to have the brand's logo grace its helmets, uniforms, and equipment.

(The growing interest in lacrosse has not been limited to the professionals: there is staggering growth in the amateur ranks. The National Federation of State High School Associations reports that participation in secondary school lacrosse has rock-eted 206% in the last ten years. As for the youngest players, the number of both leagues and players under fifteen-years-old tripled between 1999 and 2005; currently over half-a-million players are registered, and the Sporting Goods Manufacturing Association has declared lacrosse the fastest growing team sport in North America. In 2005, *Sports Illustrated* called lacrosse "the fastest growing sport in the United States."

The epicenter of this explosion of interest in the sport is the National Lacrosse League. Founded in 1985 in Kansas City, Mo., the NLL began as the brainchild of a promoter, Chris Fritz, and a former executive with the Kansas City Chiefs, Russ Cline. The two men were eager to find sources of year-round revenues for indoor sports arenas. Fritz and Cline believed that profes-sional indoor lacrosse would be financially feasible as a sport. They decided to put their idea to the test. In 1985, they cre-ated a tour of All-Stars, mostly ex-college players from Canada and the United States. The tour traveled around the U.S. and was successful in generating interest in the game: good crowds attended the exhibitions. The pair was encouraged enough to organize the Eagle Pro Box Lacrosse League. The League consisted of four teams—the Baltimore Thunder, Washington D.C. Wave, Philadelphia Wings, and the New Jersey Saints. The inaugural season of 1987 consisted of six regular games and a series of playoffs. In that first season's championship game, the Thunder defeated the Wave, 11–10.

Fritz and Cline were strategic in their placement of the original four teams, not only by locating the franchises geographically close to save on transportation expenses, but also by placing each team in a region of the country dominated by college lacrosse's historically dominant teams: the University of Virginia, Syracuse and Johns Hopkins. Fritz and Cline's marketing strategy, however, did not focus on fans of the college games, or even those who had played college lacrosse, but instead focused on the "live arena" crowd—a fan base that supported minor league hockey, professional wrestling, monster truck rallies and roller derbies.

The scene was a far cry from the elite eastern colleges that had traditionally played the sport. Fritz and Cline's extravaganzas were noisy and exciting, with video screens, music, loud announcers and images of gladiators and roaring lions. By all accounts, the first years of indoor lacrosse was more action and fighting than finesse and scoring. Not surprisingly, the reviews were not all positive. *Lacrosse Magazine*, one of the publications of seminal influence on the sport in America, editorialized that the new lacrosse league "brought out the worst human elements"— which may have referred to the fans, rather than the players.

Nevertheless, Fritz and Cline knew what they were: the Eagle League was a financial success and the seeds were sown. In 1988, it was renamed the Major Indoor Lacrosse League (MILL); in 1997, the MILL was folded into its upstart rival, the National Lacrosse League, but Fritz and Cline, both of whom were inducted into the Lacrosse Hall of Fame in 2006, retained ownership of their "baby," the Philadelphia Wings.

Of course, Fritz and Cline's incarnation of lacrosse was by no means the sport's first appearance in North America: its first press was the history written by Spanish missionaries in the 1500s who observed the game as played by Native Americans. Native Americans—Indians—called the game "baggataway." When the French Jesuit missionaries saw the wooden clubs, they declared them to resemble a bishop's staff ("*la crosse*"). The French word for the game stuck.

The bishop's staff observation, however, came from the Jesuits watching a Huron game in southeast Ontario, Canada; who knows what the game would have been called if they had watched the tribes play in the Southeastern part of what is now the United States, they would have seen the Cherokee playing with two tools, much like giant chop sticks, to pick up, pass, and carry the ball. In the Great Lakes region, tribes played with three-foot-long sticks carved at one end like a wooden spoon. In the New York region, the Iroquois played with sticks that most resembled today's, with a webbing of animal skin forming a pouch at one end.

The balls used by the Indians were most commonly made of deer skin, but whatever natural resources were at hand were used: rocks, carved wood, or hardened clay. Poles, trees, and rocks were all pressed into service as goals.

In those days, no one would have noticed Mr. Langtry's black eye: while modern lacrosse can be a very rough sport, with checks and fights, nothing can compare to those original contests, played, as they often were, to settle disputes over trading rights and hunting rights between rival tribes. (Baggataway was also believed to heal the sick and develop strong, virile men and for that reason was, and still is, called "The Creator's Game," by Native Americans.)

Imagine: often as many as *1,000 players* on each side took turns on a field that was a mile to up to *15 miles long*. The games resembled warfare: no rules (punching, hitting, tackling were all commonplace), no referees, and no boundaries. The competitions often lasted from sunrise to sunset; some were occasionally played over several days. Frequently, players would suffer severe injuries or even death.

The first non-Native Americans to play baggataway—lacrosse—were the French Canadians from Montreal who began, in the early 1800s, to organize the game into a sport with a few basic rules: the size of the field, boundaries, the length of time of a game, and the number of players on a team. These refinements may have "civilized" the game—that was the French intention—but lacrosse didn't begin to grow in popularity until it was played as a college sport.

The first university in North America to have an official lacrosse team was New York University in 1877. Lacrosse programs at private secondary schools soon followed: Phillips Academy in Andover, Mass., Phillips Exeter Academy in New Hampshire; Lawrenceville School in New Jersey. (While history documents the first women's lacrosse game at St. Leonard's School in Scotland in 1890, the first women's college team, at Bryn Mawr School, was not successfully established until 1926. Today, more women's teams play Division I lacrosse than men's teams.)

While the sport of outdoor lacrosse was growing in Canada and the northeast region of the United States, a new idea took root that would lead to the future National Lacrosse League —the development of indoor or "box" lacrosse.

Originally started by Canadians who wanted to work on their hockey skills during exceptionally cold winters, box lacrosse (named as such because it was first played in a square indoor arena) first appeared in 1930.

The sport was not easy on the participants. The original game was played on cement. (It would be another thirty years before the appearance of Astroturf.) Scooping, faking, pivoting and checking on cement often led to injuries. Yet, there was interest and excitement because indoor lacrosse features faster transitions, more scoring, more hitting, and, especially with a shot-clock, more action.

Just as the ABA challenged the NBA, and the AFL challenged the NFL, the Major Indoor Lacrosse League received a challenge in 1997 as a new ownership group created a league to rival the MILL and called it the National Lacrosse League (NLL). Initially it seemed this start-up venture would not work, however when the new owners lured the MILL's biggest stars, Gary and Paul Gait, to jump to this new league, it has to be taken seriously. This move forced the MILL's original ownership group to reconsider its options. In many ways, the MILL had not grown from being an attraction into a real league. Not only did it have a monopolistic ownership group, the league had odd rules, such as the home field advantage in the playoffs being determined by home attendance.

The NLL challenge forced a transformation which ultimately improved the league. Both management groups realized that creating rival leagues could destroy professional lacrosse;

instead, they combined forces, merged, and founded the National Lacrosse League.

Meanwhile the influence that the Gait brothers had on the sport of lacrosse during this time was staggering. At a time when pro lacrosse was struggling to maintain its existence, with players being paid $100 per game, and the league being described by some lacrosse fans as being full of "thugs" who liked to fight more than to score goals—the two Canadian brothers from Ontario, both All-Americans from Syracuse University—changed the game, and changed the fan base.

In 1991, their first year as professionals, the Gaits brought the Detroit Turbos, a first-year franchise, the NLL title. Fans saw the Gait's incredible scoring abilities and staggering accomplishments never seen before (or since) on the lacrosse pitch. (The Gaits jointly hold the record of scoring 10 goals in a single game—in a sport that sometimes does not see 10 goals scored by an entire team.)

Fans responded. As a story in the *Toronto Globe* tells it, in 1987, the only cable broadcasts for indoor lacrosse were six tape-delayed broadcasts in the Philadelphia/Baltimore. By 1992, the year after the Gait brothers arrived, 50 North American media markets were televising games, many of which were live, to over 26 million viewers.

Gary retired in April 2005 and at the opening game of the 2006 NLL season in December 2005, the Colorado Mammoth, the team he now coaches, raised Gary's jersey, No. 22, to the rafters of the Pepsi Center in Denver. It is the first retired jersey in NLL history.

After the founding of the modern NLL, the league headquarters were moved from Kansas City, Mo., to New York City, and added to the mix was a league commissioner, team management groups, and playoffs that more closely resembled the successful models of professional football, baseball, basketball and hockey.

One of the best consequences of the formation of the NLL was the expansion of the league into Canada in 1998 with the establishment of the Hamilton Raiders franchise. The Raiders soon became the Toronto Rock—and after the Rock won back-to-back national championships, Canadians embraced professional lacrosse with fervor.

Not surprisingly, the first athlete mentioned as "the greatest ever" in the history of lacrosse was a Native American, Jim Thorpe.

Thorpe was a student at the Carlisle Indian Industrial School in Pennsylvania, a controversial institution where 12,000 Native American children from more than 140 tribes were uprooted from their families and shipped to the school to be "assimilated" into a European-American culture in a practice that lasted nearly forty years—from 1879 to 1918. Jim—Jacobus Franciscus was his baptismal name and Wa-Tho-Huk, "Bright Path" was his native name—had a twin brother, Charlie, who died when the boys were eight. Angry and depressed, Jim ran away from more than one school; finally, in 1904, when he was 17, he entered the Carlisle School. He dropped out again, returned when he was 20, and began an astonishing athletic career under the tutelage of the school's coach, Glenn Scobey—"Pop"—Warner.

Pop Warner, one of the founders of modern football, decided in 1910 to drop the baseball program at the Carlisle School in favor of lacrosse. For one reason, lacrosse, a more athletic endeavor, would give Warner the chance scout players for speed, skill, endurance, and stamina that would make great football players. For another reason, baseball was, at the time, disreputable. From a January, 1910 issue of *The Arrow*, the newspaper of the Carlisle Indian Industrial School:

This school will not be represented by a base ball {sic} team the coming season. In place of base ball, lacrosse will be taken up as a school sport. This change has been considered for several years, and has been decided upon only after most thoughtful consideration. It is thought that, because of the evils of summer or—professional - base ball and the fact that many students have been lured away from school and into temptations and bad company by professional offers before they had finished school, it would be best not to develop, by encouraging base ball, an ambition in the students to become professional players...

Thorpe joined lacrosse the team; in 1912, he led Carlisle to an upset victory of then (and now) powerhouse Johns Hopkins University. That same year, Thorpe participated in the Olympics in Stockholm, Sweden. There, he won—easily—both the Pentathlon and the Decathlon, after which King Gustav V pronounced him "The Greatest Athlete in the World." (He later played both professional football and professional baseball.)

Coincidentally, there was an Olympic lacrosse competition at the 1912 Olympic Games: lacrosse had been on the roster since 1904, when the U.S. began its participation in the world event. At that time, lacrosse was foreign outside North America, and only three teams competed: one from the U.S., and two from Canada, one of which was solely composed of Mohawk Indians (the gold medal was won by the other Canadian team, the Shamrock). An English lacrosse team was fielded for the 1908 Olympics, but Canada again won the gold medal, and that was that. Lacrosse was played as an exhibition sport in three other Olympics (1928, 1932, and 1948); it has not appeared on the agenda since.

Football was also the sport of fame for the second player considered the "greatest lacrosse player ever"—Jim Brown.

In the 1950s, Brown won four varsity letters: in lacrosse (as a midfielder), football, basketball and track at Manhasset High School on Long Island. After receiving help from a local benefactor, he attended Syracuse University and dominated the lacrosse pitch, earning second-team All-American honors in 1956, and first team All-American honors in 1957. Although he would be better known for his football exploits at Syracuse and later as one of the NFL's all-time greatest players as a running back for the Cleveland Browns, Brown may have been even more talented at lacrosse than football. His last lacrosse game in 1957 may have been his greatest, when playing only the first half of the Collegiate North/South College All-Star Game, he scored five goals. It was to be his last competitive lacrosse appearance.

Brown, who still remains the only college athlete to achieve All-American honors in both lacrosse and football, told *the New York Times* in a 1985 interview, "Lacrosse is probably the best sport I ever played. There is no publicity, no pressure, just great competition...I'd rather play lacrosse six days a week, and football on the seventh."

Today, there are thousands of men and women who agree with Jim Brown: lacrosse is the best sport they've ever played. And many of those men, the lucky ones, are choosing to play professional lacrosse—but not without sacrifice or extraordinary support of their families and their employers or long hours spent traveling across North America. Professional lacrosse players do not earn enough money to rely on the sport to provide for themselves or their families: they must also have full-time employment, businesses, careers. Professional lacrosse, at best, is practiced once a week—usually on Wednesdays—and played on the weekends. The men who, for the love of the game, keep up these tough schedules are called "Weekend Warriors." These are their stories.

Dan Ladouceur

A "BIG DOG" ON AND OFF THE FIELD

A police officer was responding to a potentially dangerous situation: a stolen vehicle with the perpetrator leaving the scene at a rapid rate of speed. Dan Ladouceur and Pat Jones, his partner for the day, scrambled into their squad car and pursued the stolen car through the streets. Each car reached speeds of 110 miles per hour before the perpetrator's vehicle spun out and stopped. Ladouceur and Jones jumped from their car, pulled the thief from the stolen car, pinned him to the ground, and made the arrest.

It was an unusually bad day for the bad guy. His arresting officers, Ladouceur and Jones, members of the Durham (Toronto) Region Police Force were both professional lacrosse players.

Further, Ladouceur, who is 6'6" and 245 pounds and a defenseman for the NLL's Toronto Rock, has a reputation for partaking of what players call "the heavy stuff."

His supervisor on the police force, Sergeant Wally Wilson, says, "Dan is an enforcer on the Durham Regional Police, and he is an enforcer in the National Lacrosse League. I don't know if he's the biggest guy on the force, but he sure is the toughest. I wouldn't want to get in the ring with him."

Ladouceur admits he hasn't survived eight years in the NLL due to his scoring ability or his fancy footwork. Only two other players in the NLL (Neil Doddridge—362 minutes, and Pat Coyle—357 minutes) have more time in the penalty box. As of early 2007, Ladouceur had 356 penalty minutes in the box in 106 career games. In one game alone against Vancouver in 2003, he was tagged with a season high of 22 penalty minutes.

But Ladouceur's toughest moment was in 2005 against the Calgary Roughnecks.

"I was in a fight and I missed with an uppercut and smashed my hand into the glass," Dan says. The broken hand bothered him throughout the 2005 season, although he still suited up for 12 games and the playoffs. "It also ruined any future I may have had in hand-modeling!"

Brian Langtry laughs. "My rookie year with the Colorado Mammoth, we played against the Toronto Rock in the play-offs. In the third quarter, Ladouceur slashed across my hand. This happens all the time, but he is so strong. Later in the game I felt something was wrong. I looked at my hand. He had broken my finger. To this day, I'm not sure Dan realized that happened."

Ladouceur's reputation for fighting has not always gone over well with his wife, Angela. "In the early days she used to leave the arena whenever I got in a fight," he says. "Now she's gotten to the point where she can tolerate it. She has come to understand that it is part of the game." (He may be a bit more cautious as well: he also added that as he's gotten older, "the heavy stuff," hurts a little bit more the next day.)

While Ladouceur's reputation is as a bruiser on the lacrosse pitch, people who know him off the field say he does not fit that personality. "He is a laid-back guy," Sgt. Wilson says, "and he's great with kids. One guy on the force had a kid who played lacrosse. He would bring his kid in after work, to see Dan, and the two of them would throw the ball around in the basement. And Dan has done a lot of charity work."

Ladouceur regularly visits local schools and has recorded an anti-alcohol message that is airs on radio stations as a public service announcement in Toronto. Most recently, he coached the Ontario Pee Wees in the Pee Wee National Box Lacrosse Championships in the Iroquois Park Arena.

"Dan is a natural born leader," says Jones, who in addition to being Ladouceur's occasional crime-fighting partner, was his teammate on the Rock for 2003–2004 seasons before Jones went to Oregon to play for the Portland Lumberjax. "Everybody looks up to him, not just on the police force, but on the team as well."

Dan Ladouceur's long road to playing professional lacrosse began in Thunder Bay, Ontario when he was eight years old.

"Like any red-blooded Canadian, I played hockey," he says. "But you have to find something to do in the summer. For me, that was soccer, until some of my hockey buddies said I should try lacrosse - that it would help with hockey." He gave it a try, and became hooked with lacrosse's constant action and physical play.

Ladouceur played in the junior and senior leagues in Canada, but unlike some of the college starts coming out of the U.S., he was not drafted. Instead, he enrolled in a local community college and focused on his law enforcement career, a field he had chosen for its wide variety of work: detective work, forensics, and what was to become his specialty, tactical operations.

Ladouceur's lacrosse playing days, however, were not over. In 1998, he was invited to try out as an un-drafted walk-on with the NLL's Hamilton Raiders (later becoming the Rock). He had a "good camp," and made it down to the last cut before he was let go, an experience he describes as "agonizing."

The following year, the team again asked him to come join the training camp and try out.

"I was cheeky," Ladouceur says. "I asked the coach if it was worth my time. I didn't want to go down there and not make the team again." The coach assured him that there would be a place on the team for him if he had a good camp, so Ladouceur gave the dream one more shot. He had a strong performance in camp, one that convinced the coaching staff to add him to the roster.

Nevertheless, at the first game of his rookie season, he was not asked to suit up.

"I don't remember the final score," he says. "We played the old Baltimore franchise. We got shellacked. Something like a 21–9 loss."

The next day, when Ladouceur reported for the weekly practice session, the coach said that not only would he suit up for the next game, but that he would see some playing time in an effort to shake up the team.

"The equipment manager was caught by surprise. He didn't have a jersey for me. He went to see if he could find a jersey that fit me, and he found only one—No. 6. That became my number. I didn't have a choice in the matter."

Nor did Ladouceur have a choice in the selection of his nickname.

"I am a big guy," he says. "At 6'6", 245, I'm one of the biggest players in the league. But I didn't know I had a nickname until it was announced at the start of that first game. The announcer said, 'Dan—Big Dog—Ladouceur.' It stuck."

Big Dog lit up that first game with his aggressive defensive play. He's seen action as a member of the Toronto Rock ever since.

Lacrosse fits in well with Ladouceur's schedule as police officer with the special weapons team, a unit similar to a U.S. police SWAT team, that is called in as sharpshooters during drug and gun bust operations, or any other threats that require sharpshooters to surround, disable, and arrest multiple targets during police operations, especially when those targets are armed and dangerous.

"It takes an enormous amount of planning and teamwork, just like lacrosse," Ladouceur says.

Another aspect of his job that works out well is that as a member of the special teams, Ladouceur is required to stay in peak physical condition. The force has a gym on-site at police headquarters for strength and cardio training. Ladouceur is also required to go to the shooting range twice a week to practice with his 40-caliber Glock-22 sidearm and his M4-Colt rifle.

"He is an excellent shot," says Sergeant Wilson. "I would say he is a marksman."

Fortunately, Ladouceur has never had to fire his weapon while on duty, a good thing. "When police fire their weapons," he says, "that means something has gone wrong. We try to surround and neutralize the targets so that does not happen."

There have been times when police work has interfered with his training as a weekend warrior. As a member of the tactics team, he has a beeper, and is on-call 24/7. Over the course of his career, his beeper has gone off two or three times during Rock practices.

"I have to tell the lacrosse team, sorry, I've gotta go, and my teammates have been very understanding. For me to play in the NLL, it takes a lot of teamwork," he says of his colleagues on the police force. "Other guys at the station have to cover for me. But they know, there are always Toronto Rock tickets left at the front counter for them when they want to see a game."

Ladouceur's co-workers are not the only ones who encourage him to play in the NLL. His wife, Angela, is his consistent ally.

"I couldn't do it without Angela," he says. "In the winter, she becomes a single-parent to our daughter Madeleine because I am gone so much." And it's Madeleine who may be his biggest fan.

"She comes to all of the home games, and for the away games, she listens to the Rock games on the radio. If there is ever a time where she isn't able to hear a game, she gets very upset."

When asked to reflect on the changes in lacrosse he has seen over the years, Ladouceur immediately cites the increase in the level of competition.

"When I first started playing, several players would say they would try lacrosse for the heck of it. They didn't know if they could make a career of it, or if the NLL would last. The success and growth of the NLL has changed that. Whereas, in 1998, some of the best college players may have decided to go to graduate school or pursue 'real jobs,' now the best lacrosse players in the country are becoming NLL players. They are also more mindful of their careers and are in better shape. And the intensity level is the highest I've ever seen."

Big Dog's fondest NLL memory is a no-contest: it's the 2005 NLL Championship Game between the Toronto Rock and the Arizona Sting. Playing in front of his entire family, all his co-workers, 20,000 other fans in the Air Canada Centre in Toronto, and televisions throughout North America, Dan Ladouceur and his teammates defeated the Sting 19–13.

With a championship in his pocket, Ladouceur can approach the end of his lacrosse career, still continuing his career on the police force, but focusing his more on fighting on criminals and less on fighting his fellow laxmen on the pitch.

"I want to be able to walk away from the game in one piece," he says. "I may end up with arthritis in my hands when I'm sixty or seventy, but right now I'm fine, and I'd like to keep it that way."

Regy Thorpe

INSURANCE ON THE DEFENSE

A typical day for Regy Thorpe is like any other insurance executive—he arrives in the office, consults with his assistant, reads his e-mails, checks the paperwork submitted by insurance agents he supervises, and heads out for appointments. A regional vice-president for Mass Mutual Financial Group, Thorpe begins his day in Elbridge, N.Y., but often stops by the district office in Rochester or the regional office in Syracuse, or visits agents in Binghamton. By the end of the day, he's once again at his desk in Elbridge going over e-mails and reading insurance applications.

A typical day, but Regy Thorpe is far from a typical insurance executive—he's a thirteen-year veteran of professional lacrosse who plays year-round for Rochester, N.Y., both in the NLL, as a member of the Knighthawks, and in Major League Lacrosse (MLL), as a player for the Rattlers.

So, when not reviewing claims and setting up sales meetings, the 6'1", 240-pound Thorpe is smashing opponents against the boards and showcasing his lacrosse skills in front of thousands of paying fans in some of the biggest arenas in the country and in front of hundreds of thousands of television viewers across North America.

"He's just a regular guy," says Karen Palmer, his assistant at Mass Mutual. "Outgoing and funny, with a serious side."

"He was a tough kid," says long-time friend and fellow insurance executive, Wayne Lafluer. "I was two years older, so I never played with him, but I saw him play in high school. He was a good, solid, tough player, but it still amazes me that he blossomed into such a defensive icon as a professional. I don't know how he does it. He's thirty-five years old and not only does he go down and hammer it out with twenty-one-year-olds—you can see that they want to stay away from him."

Growing up Elbridge, Thorpe was an outstanding high school player who was recruited by nearby lacrosse powerhouse Syracuse. There was one small problem. In high school, Thorpe had been a bit too involved in lacrosse and a bit uninvolved in homework. His high school grades weren't good enough for Syracuse. Thorpe solved that hurdle by enrolling in New York's Herkimer County Community College, a two-year school with an outstanding lacrosse program.

At Herkimer, under the guidance of Coach Paul Wehrum, Thorpe had two successful years on and off the lacrosse pitch, and was named an All-American and Defensive Player of the Year.

"I have coached lacrosse, football, and wrestling—for twenty-four years and I've never seen a leader like Regy Thorpe," says Coach Wehrum, who remembers well when he recruited Thorpe in the late 1980s. "He was a tough kid, a brute, huge shoulders, and once he got running his arms and legs were like pistons. Nobody can stop him. But what sticks in my mind is the recruiting trip when he came to Herkimer. After we were done talking, he turned toward the door, put his arm around his mother, and told her this is where he wanted to go to school. After seeing that, I stopped him before he reached the door and I told him I would do everything I could to get him to attend our college. I knew he was a great player, but a big, tough kid who's gentle like that with his mother—that's a kid I'd love to coach."

After Thorpe's play at Herkimer, Syracuse came calling again, and this time Thorpe's academic performance met the standard. At Syracuse, Thorpe made an immediate impression: he was named co-captain of the 1993 NCAA Championship team, for which he garnered an Honorable Mention All-American. And even though he had spent his first two college years elsewhere, the Orangemen elected Thorpe captain his senior year.

"I was invited to the locker room prior to Syracuse playing Johns Hopkins in the NCAA semifinals," says coach Wehrum, "Everyone was tense. The coaches were sharing their scouting report on Johns Hopkins. It was a daunting, intimidating list of point scorers, All-Americans, tournament MVPs. Then someone from the Syracuse team spoke up from the back and said, 'So what? We've got Regy.' That's the type of kid he was."

At Syracuse, Thorpe selected one of the stranger majors of choice for a lacrosse player: Non-Violent Conflict and Change.

"I know it sounds odd," says Thorpe, "but the major is part social work, part mediator, part political science. That's what I enjoyed. I considered becoming a social worker or a parole office. I like helping people. The problem is, the money wasn't there and I had a family to support." (At Syracuse, he had met and married his wife, Amy.)

A career came along when Thorpe saw an advertisement recruiting insurance salesmen for Mutual of Omaha. He applied for the job, was accepted, and began a career in insurance sales. With his extroverted personality, he was successful, and in just over a year, was promoted to management. Shortly thereafter, his daughter, Ella, was born.

Lacrosse was on hold. "I did want to play," he says. "I was invited to try out for the Buffalo Bandits, but due to my classes I could not make the physical—my work and my family responsibilities had to come first."

Then, fate intervened and provided another opportunity. The city of Rochester obtained an NLL franchise, and the new coach, Barry Powless (a former Syracuse University lacrosse stand-out, and a part-time actor who has appeared in, among other movies, *The Last of the Mohicans*), called Thorpe and asked him to try out.

Once again, Thorpe had to make a choice between his family and lacrosse. This time, for one important night, he chose lacrosse.

Amy was pregnant with the couple's second child, and nearing her delivery time.

"That was the era before we all had cell phones," says Thorpe. "We knew the baby could come any day, but we didn't know when for sure." The couple talked it over, and agreed Thorpe could play in a scrimmage against the Buffalo Bandits.

"I had to go if I wanted to make the team," he recalls.

During what Thorpe described as a very rough scrimmage, he was in the penalty box when he saw an assistant for the Rochester team waving, trying to get his attention. Amy had gone in to labor and was headed toward the hospital.

Thorpe finished the game, dressed quickly, and raced to the hospital, but he arrived too late. Amy had already given birth to their son, Gale.

"Yeah, I still get crap about that sometimes," he chuckles.

The sacrifice was worth it—at least according to Regy. He made the team and played in for the Rochester Knighthawks in its inaugural year in 1995. At the beginning of the 2007 season, Thorpe is the only original member of the team remaining. He has played in every Knighthawks postseason game and is on almost every franchise all-time team record including penalty minutes, loose balls, and most games played.

Yet, after he made the team, and his second child was born, he was promoted by Mutual of Omaha into management— you would think it would be smooth sailing, but not exactly. "It was tough in the early years," he explains. "You have to remember we only got paid $100 a game, sometimes $150 a game and not all the expenses were reimbursed. Actually it probably cost money to play professional lacrosse."

"We all like to say we'll play the game for free, but the truth is, I probably wouldn't have played as long as I have if I did not make some money," he says. With his full-time job, Thorpe sees his lacrosse salary as supplemental income often going into his children's college fund, he and his wife's retirement fund, or when changes are needed around the house.

Says Thorpe, "I hope one day, maybe by the time my son Gale is old enough to play, I'll see lacrosse become the fifth major team sport in America with salaries over $100,000 so pro players can make a comfortable living."

While racking up many Knighthawk team records through the years, Thorpe has also gained the respect of his competitors and is considered a trailblazer in the National Lacrosse League.

Says former New York Saint Armando Polanco, "Some coaches used to take the quick outdoor lacrosse defensemen— the scoop and run defensemen, and convert them to indoor lacrosse players. Regy Thorpe is a guy who opened the door for big physical guys like me by proving you could be a big physical defensemen who gets a body on people every time they come down the floor, and make it in the league by playing that style. He changed the way they play defense in the NLL. What can I say? He's a legend who has gained a lot of respect from the other players."

Nevertheless, Thorpe competes in the smallest media market and one of the NLL's smallest arenas—Rochester's Blue Cross Arena has only 13,500 seats—and his recognition does not carry him very far.

"We're like the Green Bay Packers of the National Football League," says Thorpe. "But I love playing for Rochester and I love the small arena."

What does the future hold for Thorpe? "Every year I ask my kids if I should keep playing, and every year they say yes."

During the 2005 campaign, Thorpe suffered a potentially career-ending ACL injury in his knee. During 2006, not only did he return for a successful season, he was named the NLL Comeback Player of the Year.

For now, Thorpe is focusing on his job at Mass Mutual Financial Group, including hiring and training agents, and working diligently on his company's compliance to the New York State's insurance laws. "Fortunately, our company is rated very high in compliance," he says. "If we ever do have disciplinary actions, I have to be involved with that too." However, when he is not on the road, and in the Elbridge offices, Thorpe heads to the gym during lunch hour to lift weights. "When I can't do that, I work-out right after work. Often I work out with my kids who are now old enough to lift weights."

That does not include all of Thorpe's extracurricular activities. He is an assistant coach at Jordan-Elbridge High School and is also the player-assistant coach for the MLL outdoor lacrosse franchise in Rochester.

"Right now, my focus is playing," he says. "One day, though, I'd love to coach in the NLL." He'll be a good coach, predicts Thorpe's teammate Marshall Abrams, who was coached by Thorpe in high school.

"Regy is a players' coach," says Abrams. "He is intense, but he is also cool under pressure. When he was my coach, he made sure we were prepared for everything, and he helped us minimize the errors."

And what if it didn't go as planned, as often it does in high school lacrosse? "He wasn't the kind of guy to throw his clipboard or yell at the players. If you screwed up, he would talk to you like a fellow player, tell you how to do things differently the next time."

However, before he undertakes coaching, Thorpe has a few more insurance emails to shuffle through.

Ryan McNish

CORPORAL PUNISHMENT

The management of the Calgary Roughnecks took its time re-signing the stand-out defenseman, Ryan McNish, at the beginning of the 2007 season. But not for the usual reasons of contract negotiations—McNish is one of the highest regarded defensive players in the National Lacrosse League.

No, the Roughnecks were waiting to hear if McNish would be headed to Afghanistan. Like all weekend warriors, he has a job away from pro lacrosse, and McNish's job is as an active corporal with the Canadian Air Force's 408th Tactical Helicopter Squadron based out of Edmonton, Alberta.

Eventually, McNish learned that his unit would not be placed on a state of "high readiness" for several months—long enough for the 6'2", 230-pound defenseman nick-named "Corporal Punishment"—to compete on the NLL's indoor fields.

"I am quite prepared, in fact, I want to fight for my country," McNish says. "Why else would I enlist for a long-term engagement?" (His commitment is for twenty years.)

Nevertheless, the delay in shipping to a combat zone is a fortunate circumstance for McNish who treasures every moment where he lives his dream of playing professional lacrosse.

McNish was raised in Winnipeg, Manitoba, a province that had not yet had a resident drafted by the National Lacrosse League. Following the family tradition, McNish played baseball and "dabbled" in rugby and hockey.

"There was too much standing around in baseball," says McNish. "I wanted to play a sport with more action that was more physical." McNish says his father, a former high school baseball star, was disappointed at first over his decision to choose lacrosse over baseball, and his mother stopped going to the games because it was "too violent." Now, his parents are high biggest fans. His mother also acts as one of his scouts. She scans the internet, researches the best players for each upcoming game and calls her son, giving him tips on the biggest scorers, assist men, and the players to watch.

McNish signed up with the armed forces when he was 17 and still in high school. By the time he graduated, he had completed basic training and was a member of the reserves. After graduation, he began his military career.

"I was looking for a trade, a job, and a career and I was interested in aviation," McNish says. "The army was a perfect fit."

McNish scored well on the aptitude test, and that gave him some choices, one of which landed him in the 408th Tactical Helicopter Squadron.

At that point in his life, lacrosse was a hobby and a passion, but he harbored no thought of playing pro. His high school teams had won a few local provisional championships, but that was "bush league" compared to the quality of players and coaches from the high schools in the lacrosse hotbed of Ontario.

Then, early in his military enlistment, McNish was stationed in Bordon, Ontario, and had the opportunity to play lacrosse for the Burling Chiefs in the Ontario Lacrosse Junior A Division. There, he was coached by Jeff Dowling, a man who would eventually become assistant coach of the Calgary Roughnecks. After a year in the juniors, McNish was selected in the ninth round of the NLL Draft by the Ottawa Rebel.

"I was drafted late, but I was overwhelmed to be drafted at all," he says. "I was told I was the first person ever to be drafted from Manitoba."

Unfortunately, his euphoria was short-lived. He could not work out a travel schedule from the military base.

After the Ottawa team folded, McNish's rights were acquired by the Toronto Rock. This time, McNish was able to attend camp and performed admirably. However, when it came to committing for the entire season, he was not able, once again, to work out his schedule with the military.

"It was frustrating to know that I had the ability to play, but couldn't," he says. "In the military I was a new guy. The army doesn't want a new guy gallivanting around North America."

The NLL career of McNish could have ended there, but fortunately, in 2005, Terry Sanderson, the coach of the Toronto Rock, did McNish a tremendous favor by trading his rights to the Calgary Roughnecks. There, he was reunited with Jeff Dowling.

"Sanderson didn't need to do that," McNish says. "He had a father in the military and he had a soft spot in his heart for young men who serve their country. I'm not sure Toronto got a good deal, but the coach felt that I deserved an opportunity to play, even if it wasn't for the Toronto Rock."

McNish made a quick impression on Calgary, both as a good defenseman, and as a defender who will not back down from a fight. After an early season brawl with tough 6'2", 230-pound Tim O'Brien of the Toronto Rock, *Edmonton Sun* writer Scott Zerr, who has mentioned the young McNish more than once in his columns, christened him, "the early fan favorite."

"He's a big dude," says Colorado's Brian Langtry. "I wouldn't mess with him."

"Corporal Punishment" had yet another roadblock. After ten games in an outstanding 2005 rookie season (he tallied two goals, three assists and 19 penalty minutes), McNish was playing a game against the Rock when his plant foot caught on some loose carpet near the goal, skidded, and caught again. McNish collapsed face first in the crease of his own goal.

"The goalie was shouting 'Get up! Get up!' I was yelling back 'I'm injured! I'm injured!' "

McNish tore his ACL and required reconstructive surgery. It worked, thanks to surgeon Dr. David Reid of the Edmonton Oilers hockey team. Dr. Reid replaced McNish's ACL with that of a cadaver, and McNish went on to have an outstanding sophomore season in 2006.

For McNish fans, it's not the goals, assists, and tough defense that brings excites. It's the fights. Throughout the 2006 season, internet bloggers—who also call him "McSquish"—and fans have been swapping McNish stories.

A favorite is a fight in February of 2006. On this night, Calgary squared off against its conference rival, the Edmonton Rush, at the Calgary's Saddledome. In a back-and-forth game that saw several lead changes, Jamey Bowen's power play goal for the Rush put Edmonton on top 8–7. And tempers erupted.

McNish squared off in a fist-fight with Chris Stachniak, the 6'2", 210-pound defenseman for the Rush. After a few wild punches from both sides that mostly missed their targets, McNish connected with five straight punches to the Stachniak's face, knocking out the defenseman and leaving him on his back on the Saddledome turf. Exuberant with his victory, McNish climbed the glass to receive the standing ovation of the cheering fans. Edmonton won the game, 12–11, but the fight was the highlight of the evening.

Ryan considers himself a "stay-at-home" defenseman, who does not get into the scoring action, and as an enforcer.

"Yeah, fights are part of the game," he says. "I don't mind it." He says occasionally a coach will give him a tap on the shoulder to get rough with certain players, but usually it does not work that way. McNish is watchful to make sure other teams do not "take liberties" with Calgary's star players like Kaleb Toth or Tracey Kelusky.

But while fighting is part of the game, McNish said he holds no grudges against his combatants. "Sometimes you fight during the game, and go have beers with them after the game."

McNish says the highlight of the 2006 season was on St. Patrick's Day, when, in a game against Edmonton, he scored two goals in what was to be a 16–9 victory for the Roughnecks. "It was great because a lot of my family and friends were there to see it," he says.

McNish's intensity on the lacrosse pitch translates to his job as a systems technician for his helicopter unit, where he works on the CH146-Griffins. Says McNish, "When a truck becomes disabled it will end up on the side of the road. If a helicopter becomes disabled, it can crash, a pilot can die. We take apart the helicopter and examine every piece before we certify it to fly."

The double-life creates a tough schedule for McNish.

"It is tricky," he says. "I take off two days for Christmas and that is it. All of my annual leave is dedicated to playing professional lacrosse." While the Edmonton Rush franchise is closer to the base, McNish enjoys playing for Calgary and does not mind the three-and-a-half hour drive to practices and home games.

The army is supportive of McNish's lacrosse career and there is an *esprit de corps* that pervades the unit. Fellow servicemen attend his games and he is often approached by others who ask, "Aren't you that guy who plays lacrosse?"

For now, "Corporal Punishment" is home, balancing the two major activities of his life. But the military comes first, and someday, that may mean deployment to Afghanistan.

Richard Morgan

KEEPING THE BEER COLD

"Keeping the beer cold." That's how Richard Morgan describes his job. Sooner or later, the meat cooler at Albertson's overheats, water leaks onto the floor, the staff moves the product to other coolers to avoid spoilage, and the store calls a service technician from Equipment Wholesalers.

"The problems are never the same," Morgan says. "Sometimes the evaporator doesn't work, sometimes it's a blown fan, sometimes the frame on the door doesn't close properly. "

This Equipment Wholesalers service technician is not the typical, recently graduated high-school technician with an interest in electricity and plumbing. This technician is a 27-year-old graduate of Boise State University who stands an intimidating 6'8" and weighs 260 pounds. When he's not fixing the coolers, he's a defenseman for the NLL franchise in Portland, Ore., the Lumberjax.

Morgan was the first player signed by Portland and he started off his Lumberjax career with a bang. Although he is the big guy on the back-line, he is a prolific scorer on offense. He tallied 10 goals and 11 assists in his first year, and scored the first-ever franchise goal against the Arizona Sting in the team's first game.

On the Lumberjax, he was reunited with his brothers, Dave and Pete. The very large trio (Dave is 6'10" and Pete is 6'6"), who may remind hockey fans of the "Hanson Brothers" from the movie *Slapshot,* are known as the "Tall Trees" of the Lumberjax.

"I can't tell those Morgan guys apart, they are all giants," laughs Colorado's Brian Langtry. "Richard? He's like seven feet tall. I don't mess with him."

It was not clear that lacrosse would be a path that Morgan would take in his career. A talented basketball player, Morgan played professional basketball in Europe before turning his career to professional lacrosse.

Growing up in Port Coquitlam, British Columbia, Richard dreamed of obtaining an athletic scholarship to attend college, and he did, but not in lacrosse. Playing center/forward for a regional Canadian high school basketball team, he was discovered at a tournament in Las Vegas.

"There weren't many scholarship opportunities in lacrosse," he says, "and I liked playing basketball. After the tournament, I got some interest from Division I schools to play basketball in the States. I had a few trips lined up, the first of which was Boise State. After I went to Boise, met the coach and visited the campus, I knew I wanted to go there."

In his four years at Boise State, Morgan appeared in 113 games for the Broncos, scored 677 points, grabbed 326 rebounds and shot 50.6 percent from the field. He is probably best remembered in Boise when, as a freshman in 1998, he contributed to an upset of the No. 15-ranked Washington Huskies at the Rainbow Classic in Hawaii. Media outlets at the time reported that a freshman center came off the bench in the second half to lead the Broncos on a 17–0 run, and erased a first half-deficit to defeat the Huskies in the biggest upset of the tournament. The freshman was Richard Morgan.

At Boise State, lacrosse was offered only as a club sport. "They weren't very good," Morgan says. "Most of the players could not pass or catch, but I thought it would be fun." However, his basketball coach saw things differently. "He didn't want me getting injured. He said no lacrosse. If I had played club lacrosse, I would have lost my basketball scholarship."

So what does the lacrosse enthusiast do upon graduation? Play lacrosse? Wrong.

"My older brother Pete played professional basketball in Europe for six years. I thought I'd give it a try." Morgan took his skills to the professional basketball league in Greece and signed a three-year contract to be paid $50,000, $70,000 and $120,000.

"It was one of the top leagues, but the franchise was in shambles," says Morgan. "I did get paid, but I had to force it out of them."

Under the Greek system, which allows only two players from North America per team, Richard was more valuable than he realized. "I was born in Wales. I have dual citizenship and the Greeks counted me as Welsh."

During the summer of 2003, while back in North America, Richard watched Pete play for the Western Lacrosse Association in Canada and the NLL's Vancouver Ravens. After a couple of games, he "got the itch," and started playing lacrosse again.

"I was getting the feeling back. One day, I was stretching during warm-ups before a game, and I had a moment where it all came together" he says. "I loved lacrosse, and basketball was not much fun anymore. I decided right at that moment that I wasn't going back to Europe. I was done playing pro basketball."

Although Morgan had made the commitment to lacrosse, he didn't get a quick break. He went first to the NLL's Anaheim franchise that was struggling to stay in the league.

"My first year we won only one game and went 1–15," he says. "However, during the second year we had a coaching change and ended up improving to 5–11. I thought we were starting to play better. Then, the team ran out of money."

The shortfall of Anaheim's funds gave Morgan an unexpected leverage. Although failed franchises usually lead to disbursal drafts, Morgan had some unpaid expenses. A significant part of the arbitration negotiation with the league resulted in Morgan gaining the right to be a free agent.

"I wanted to live where I played lacrosse," he says. "The obvious team was the then-new Portland Lumberjax. The Pacific Northwest is right between my wife Heather's family—my in-laws—and my parents in British Columbia.

Since Morgan is one of the only Lumberjax who lives in the Portland area year-round, he is often the face of the franchise.

"He is a phenomenal player, but what is more important, he is dedicated to the community," says Portland Owner/President Angela Batinovich. "Richard is a dream for community relations. He's been involved in school programs and team try-outs, and he gives kids private lessons."

In the off-season, after his debut year with the Lumberjax in 2006, Morgan accepted a challenge from the Lumberjax's community relations office, Adam Bysouth, to run in the Portland Marathon to raise money for Oregon lacrosse.

"I thought it was a great cause," said Morgan. "In Canada, I didn't have an opportunity to play organized outdoor lacrosse in high school. Oregon is trying to raise money to help lacrosse become a sanctioned high school sport. That would lead to a huge growth in lacrosse in this region. And as far as the running goes, I've been into sports my whole life, and consider myself mentally strong."

On the day of the 2006 marathon in Portland, the weather was in the 50s and 60s—perfect for long-distance running. Morgan lined up with the other runners, took off—and finished what was his first marathon in 4 hours 30 minutes and 31 seconds, besting over half of the participants, to hit the line at 3,351st out of 7,705 finishers.

To put Morgan's achievement into perspective, Jay Silvanima, the race director for the Tallahassee Marathon, says Morgan's time and effort is "too incredible to believe."

"I've never seen anyone 6'8" run any distance, let alone a marathon," says Silvanima. "Running is hard on your ankles and knees, and especially for larger people with more body weight. Richard almost broke four hours. Only twenty percent of first-time marathoners break four hours, and most of those are kids who run competitively in high school, or have running-type bodies. Richard Morgan does not have a running-type body, but he has commitment and determination."

In the meantime, back to keeping the beer cold.

"It's true I have to take a job to pay the bills, but this is a real opportunity with a growing company," Morgan says of his day-job. "Equipment Wholesalers has been great in training me, showing me how the company works."

Morgan has negotiated to continue his simultaneous career in professional lacrosse. In exchange for weekends off, he supplies the boss with a steady stream of Lumberjax tickets.

Gavin Prout

IT'S A FAMILY AFFAIR

Gavin Prout, a forward with the Colorado Mammoth, usually has long days. He rises a 7 a.m., commutes an hour to work, works until 5:30, commutes the hour back home—to a gym—works out for ninety minutes, and finally, around 9 p.m., settles down for dinner. Not the typical life of a professional athlete.

Prout's company, Special Benefits Insurance Services, in Toronto, is rolling out a new marketing campaign and Prout is "burning up the phone lines," calling graphic designers and printers to obtain cost quotes. If that were not enough, it's Friday, a day when the company is short-staffed, and Prout is picking up telephones, answering customer's questions, pitching a few new products to potential customers, and working on the company website.

Special Benefits writes insurance policies for individual health and individual dental plans; the majority of its clients are Canadians who, in the process of changing or losing jobs, no longer have an employer's health insurance.

Prout is what he seems at first glance—a son following in his father's footsteps, managing the family business, a venture that includes his brother Barry John, and his sister, Nicole.

But he is also a professional lacrosse player, leaving Toronto on the weekends to play for the NLL's Colorado Mammoth as a forward. And what player he is. In his first five years in the National Lacrosse League, Prout racked up 149 career goals and 267 career assists. In his "career year" with the Mammoth in 2006, the 5'10", 185-pound Prout appeared in all sixteen games regular season games, and scored 29 goals and 64 assists. In addition, he scored an amazing 10 goals and 15 assists during Colorado's successful 2006 play-off run that ended with the NLL Championship, a victory that garnered Prout the Most Valuable Player award for the game.

This well-deserved success, however, was not without a journey of significant detours. Prout began his collegiate lacrosse career as a Laker at Mercyhurst College in Erie, Pa.

"Nobody recruited Canadians that much," he says, "probably because there were a limited amount of scholarships, and they didn't want to gamble on Canadian kids who played box lacrosse that only uses one hand. The outdoor game is a little foreign to us."

But Prout made an impression on Mercyhurst coach Pete Ginnegar, who saw him play in the World Lacrosse Games in Japan on Canada's junior team in 1996. Coach Ginnegar invited him for a try-out and then offered him a scholarship.

"I never figured out what a 'Laker' was exactly." Gavin says, "The mascot was a really buff guy. That's all I know." Gavin would not get four years to figure out the riddle. After his freshman year as a Laker, Mercyhurst College, which had a limited number of slots for Division I schools, decided to elevate hockey to Division I status and demote lacrosse to Division II.

"The rug was pulled out from under us," says Prout. "There were five or six of us who had come from Canada just to play Division I lacrosse. We thought it was over."

Not quite. Coach Ginnegar accepted the lacrosse job at Gannon University right down the street in Erie and took several of his best players with him, including Gavin Prout. Prout was then chosen captain of the Gannon University Knights.

"We had a great season. It was an up-and-coming program," Gavin says. "The year before we came, the team was ranked No. 51 in the country, and after the first year we were No. 29. We had the potential of being a top-twenty team, which was unheard of for any of Gannon's sports programs."

Sadly, the athletic director at Gannon decided the expense of a national lacrosse program was too exorbitant. He cut the program after Prout's first and only season with the Knights.

"Then, I got a call from coach Dave Cottle of the Loyola Greyhounds in Maryland," Prout says. "I thought it was somebody's idea of a joke, but he asked if I was interested in coming down for a try-out. I sent him some game tapes and traveled to Maryland."

The try-out did not go as well as Prout would have hoped. Two of the assistant coaches watched his work-outs and thought he was too small, not athletic enough, and wouldn't fit well into the program. Cottle disagreed, overruled his assistants, and offered Prout a full scholarship. Cottle, whose work at the University of Maryland is now legendary, clearly saw something his assistants did not: as a Greyhound, Prout achieved honorable mention as an All-American in 2000, made first team All-American in 2001, and was named captain of the Greyhounds.

So far, so good. And then, what looked like opportunity became a disaster: he was drafted by the NLL's New York Saints. His play was outstanding—in 2002, he made the All-Rookie team, was named an NLL All-Star, and made second team All-Pro—but the franchise was in trouble. Prout describes his time there as "miserable."

According to Prout, the franchise did not promote the team and, plagued by financial problems, management failed to reimburse players for expenses or pay on time. The shortage of money also created "ridiculous" schedules that had the team arriving early in the morning on the day of a game to conduct camps, and give interview and autograph sessions, with no time to eat, rest, or prepare for that night's game.

The financial shortfalls also resulted in the team being evicted from hotels, and of promised game-day transportation that would never arrive. Prout also says the Saints management did not attend to the necessary international travel documents needed for the Canadian players.

"We would cross the border or go through customs at airports, and it would take four or five hours because we didn't have the proper visas, we only had temporary visas," Prout says. "Traveling was very difficult."

All of this culminated into one of the darker moments in the NLL. In Prout's final season with the Saints, he entered the locker room, minutes away from taking the field against the Philadelphia Wings, only to encounter his angry teammates, ready to strike. In addition to other problems, they hadn't been paid in two months.

"The owner was there, and took aside a few of us, the captain and the assistant captains," says Prout. "He made a bunch of promises that we would get paid and things would get better. We went back and told the rest of the team, and encouraged everyone to play. They did. Things got better for a couple of weeks, and then, that was it."

The Saints folded at the end of the season—but not before a minority owner, Charlie Russo, stepped up and opened his own checkbook to make sure everyone was fully paid and all expenses were reimbursed. "That guy is a truly class act," says Prout.

The folding of the Saints franchise left Prout an unrestricted free agent. He immediately became a heavily courted prospect by the other teams in the league.

"It was like going from the cellar to the penthouse. Everyone contacted me, and wanted to show their facilities—Calgary, Colorado, Toronto, Buffalo and Philadelphia. I traveled around the country to talk with management of the different teams. Everyone put his best foot forward. It was a fun time in my career."

Prout chose the Colorado Mammoth. The franchise was already on the upswing, and the team needed just a few pieces of the puzzle to win an NLL championship. With Prout in the line-up, they did just that in 2006. But a potential championship was not the major reason Prout went to the mile-high city.

"I wanted to play with Gary Gait," says Prout of the all-time lacrosse legend and Mammoth player and later coach. "I'd played against him, but I'd never played with him."

Gary Gait was the primary draw for Gavin Prout to select the Mammoth, but the mile-high city of Denver has its own appeal for a professional athlete.

"Denver is a sports town," says Prout. "There are huge crowds for monster truck rallies, skateboarding, and—obviously—for NLL lacrosse." In Denver, unlike New York, fans on the street recognize their star players and ask for autographs, a phenomenon the unassuming Prout says "is kind of neat."

And then, too, Gavin gets to be a teammate with his close childhood friend, Gee Nash, the Mammoth's starting goalie. The men are so close that teammates have nicknamed them "Starsky and Hutch." One of Nash's rituals is to have Prout be the last player to shoot against him before the beginning of the game.

"It's his ritual, not mine," says Prout. "But if I can be a part of something that will make him better, or allow him to prepare for the game, I'll be glad to do it." So, does he try to score during this ritual with his friend? "Nope, I just try to lob them into his chest," says Prout. "Once I accidentally whipped one in the corner and scored, and I received the most horrific glare imaginable. I could see it behind the mask. I'll never do that again, but in my defense, the stick hooked."

Fellow Mammoth teammate Brian Langtry says, "Gavin is a playmaker. It doesn't matter if he is double or triple-teamed with guys draped all over him. He just makes plays happen.

He's Mr. Machismo. He has honor and you don't test his honor. Gavin isn't the biggest guy, but like Gordie Howe in hockey, he's a guy who can score—and fight."

Meanwhile, when he's back home in Toronto running the family business, it's not all serious. "I get to schmooze the clients a lot, which means I get out of the office to entertain at Maple Leaf hockey games, Blue Jay baseball games and Toronto Rock lacrosse games, well, not the Rock—those are the same nights I'm playing for the Mammoth. My brother gets to take the clients to the Rock games. We both are doing out part as ambassadors for the league. Clients come out watch the games, and end up buying season tickets."

And insurance. Like Langtry says, Prout's a playmaker.

Kasey Beirnes

ZAMBONI DRIVER

Would anyone guess that the guy who drives the Zamboni at the local skating rink is a professional athlete?

Enter Kasey Beirnes.

"It's the dream of every Canadian kid—to drive the Zamboni between periods in a hockey game. I get to do that as part of my job," says Beirnes, who works for the recreational complexes of Center Wellington and Elora, in Ontario.

"Sometimes, though, it can be embarrassing. Sometimes, you forget to put enough water in the machine, or the water runs out. Then, the machine makes a horrible scraping noise across the ice, the crowd boos the Zamboni driver, the teams get annoyed, and you have to stop and reload."

Beirnes is not used to getting booed—unless it is from the fans of an opposing team when he's competing as a star forward and starting captain for the NLL's Minnesota Swarm.

As a young Canadian who dreamed of playing professional lacrosse, Kasey Beirnes took an unusual road to achieve his goal. While studying in college for a degree in recreation, he played for the Elora Mohawks of the Canadian Lacrosse Association's Junior B Indoor League.

"I could have played A league, but the A teams were too far away," he says. "I knew I would have more fun playing with my friends, close to home."

He had five outstanding seasons with the Mohawks, but he was not easily discovered by the NLL. "My break came when one of the coaches of an opposing team who had some connections with the NLL acted as a scout," Beirnes says. "He identified me as someone who could play at the NLL level, and I began getting calls from teams, asking if I was interested in playing pro. It was exciting."

As draft day 2001 approached, several teams expressed interest in Beirnes.

"If I'd had my choice, it would have been the Toronto Rock, because it is well established and close to home. But honestly, I would have been happy to have been drafted by anyone." The winners were the Columbus (Ohio) Landsharks, who selected Beirnes in the third round—he was twenty-eighth over-all pick in the draft.

"Looking back, it was probably good I was selected by Columbus," he says. "Playing in the NLL was definitely a step above playing in the Junior B League, and I had to learn an entirely new system. The Landsharks were a young team. Many of the kids had never played in the NLL and there weren't as many veterans taking up the spots on the roster."

The lack of professional depth on the team gave Beirnes the chance to be assistant captain. Furthermore, in his first two pro seasons, he played all thirty-two regular season games, scored 57 goals and made 48 assists.

While Beirnes enjoyed a successful start to his career on the field, off the field, the situation was not ideal.

"The Columbus franchise had trouble getting fans, and we kept seeing cutbacks off the field," he says. "Unless we had to, we never flew to games. We took the bus. For home games we had a bus pick us up in Ontario and we rode ten hours to Columbus. It's hard to play well when you spend that much time traveling." Nevertheless, if the bus rides did not provide the most optimum preparation for playing lacrosse, long trips created a more close-knit team.

And then came the trip from hell.

"Call this the growing pains of the league, but we knew we were in trouble one weekend when the bus that came to pick us up looked different," Beirnes says. "It was a 'sleeper' bus. It had beds. We traveled ten hours to Columbus to play a home game. We played terribly. We showered, got on the bus, drove to New Jersey for an away game. We spent the night on the bus. Played the next night in New Jersey and played terribly again. Then, we spent the night on the bus and drove back to Ontario. We spent forty hours on the bus that weekend. Everyone who was there remembers it has the marathon trip."

While the team usually played well, lacrosse was not gaining in popularity in Columbus, a fact that made the team nervous.

"More and more often, we heard rumors the owners were selling the team," Beirnes says. "It finally happened. We were bought by a group in Arizona that also owned the NHL's Phoenix Coyotes. We were relieved."

Beirnes moved to Arizona for the 2004 season. There, he worked part-time for the Arizona organization.

"We Canadians are only allowed a work visa for one company," he says. "I couldn't get a second job, except within the same company, the Arizona Sting. So, I worked in the office, along with a few other Canadian players, helping to make phone calls, selling season tickets."

Hard to envision a pro in the National Football League cold-calling potential fans, right?

In 2004, his first year with the Sting, Beirnes had a breakout season that firmly established him in the league—33 goals, 29 assists and 61 loose balls. He played in all sixteen games. He was clearly en route to a fantastic career with the Sting—until the first game of the 2005 season.

"It was in the second quarter of the first game of the season. I was running down the field and I felt a pop in my ankle. I went down," Beirnes recalls. "I was helped off the field, and I thought it was nothing. I tried to play some more and it happened again."

Everyone, including the Sting staff, thought it was a routine ache and pain of playing in the NLL. However, after a short lay-off and another attempt at practicing, it happened again. It was later diagnosed as a dislocated ankle tendon snapping out of place. Reconstructive surgery ended his season.

"It was terrible," he says. "I played two preseason games and that was it. I like to call it my 'Curt Schilling' injury. Except playing lacrosse, you have to be a lot more mobile than pitching a baseball."

During his extended rehab, however, Beirnes had a "kind of falling out with [Sting] management." So, he was not too surprised when, while home in Ontario, he received a call from his Arizona bosses, informing him he'd been traded to the Minnesota Swarm.

Minnesota had placed high hopes on the addition of Beirnes. He did not disappoint.

Beirnes would finish the 2006 season playing in fifteen games, tallying 24 goals and 28 assists. He was also the main factor that led Minnesota to make franchise history by going to the play-offs for the first time.

"When I first started playing for the Swarm, other teams were not that worried about us," he says. "Now, teams are beginning to respect us. I like playing for the Swarm. It is another young team. We aren't packed with superstars. We're unpredictable. Anybody can score at any time."

But Beirnes has not forgotten where he came from—and still enjoys working at home in Elora.

"You would never know he was a professional lacrosse player," says his supervisor Matt Tucker. "He is not the type to brag about his accomplishments. We live in a small community and everyone knows he plays." At home, Beirnes help arrange practice fields and consults with the scheduling when lacrosse training camps come to town. He also advises aspiring young lacrosse players who want to learn what it takes to play in the National Lacrosse League.

"He truly is an ambassador for the sport of lacrosse," Tucker says. "He is friendly, outgoing, and well-respected in the community."

He's respected on the field as well.

"Kasey is a very good player and very clever," says Marshall Abrams of the Rochester Knighthawks. "He's got great hand-eye coordination, and is very tricky. No matter what we do, it seems whenever we play him he finds a way to get one or two goals."

And still drive a Zamboni.

Del Halladay

WINEMAKER ON THE PITCH

It is a quiet morning in the Okanagan Valley, 300 miles east of Vancouver, British Columbia. After running and pumping iron at the gym, Del Halladay heads to work to crush pears with his wife, Miranda.

Del and Miranda own and operate Elephant Island Orchard Wines—(the terrain is not an island and needless to say, elephants are not indigenous to Canada)—a farm that produces prize-winning dessert wines from its cherries, apples, apricots, pears, currants, and grapes.

"All eleven of our varieties of wine sell quite well," Halladay says. "We tweak the volume up and down every year, depending on sales. Our most consistent best seller is our apricot dessert wine, followed by the dry black currant wine. The apricot wine has a very distinctive apricot flavor. The black currant wine has a tartness our customers enjoy."

The winery business works well for Halladay, as the season for most of the planting, growing, harvesting, and fermentation is between May and October 15, a time that fits neatly in opposition to his schedule as a member of the Portland Lumberjax of the National Lacrosse League.

"I had to give up outdoor lacrosse," he says. "We are too busy in the summer. But our winery schedule works great for the NLL season. Training camp is usually in November. We're through by then."

The 5'11", 185-pound forward, one of the league's veteran players, made his NLL debut in 1998, in another wine country, the Finger Lakes region of New York. There, he played for the Syracuse Smash; in two seasons, he played 24 games, had 40 goals and 46 assists.

Nice work, but in professional lacrosse, a weekend warrior still needs a day job.

"Miranda and I didn't have anything going," Del says. "Then, we thought about pursuing her grandfather's dream of opening a fruit distillery."

However, after reviewing other business operations in the area, and consulting the Canadian federal regulations and licensing for businesses selling alcoholic products, they changed their mind, and decided on a winery.

"Miranda's grandmother allowed us to build on her land," he says. "We put together a business model after visiting some local wineries, and then approached financial institutions for a loan. At the time, there were no fruit wine makers in the region, and we saw an opportunity to be successful in a niche marketplace."

There is not much of a lacrosse presence at the winery—lacrosse sticks are not used to prop up vines or fruit trees—and there is not a lacrosse net to be seen.

"He doesn't have any memorabilia at the winery per se," says winery employee Doug Weddell, "but there are a couple of newspaper articles under glass at the gift shop."

Halladay's career in lacrosse began in junior lacrosse for the Esquimalt Legion. He then went off to play college lacrosse at Loyola of Maryland, where he earned a degree in communications and advertising in 1995. Three years later, he was a rookie for the Syracuse Smash and scored 22 goals with 25 assists. Halladay literally became a "journeyman" player—moving around from team to team—he played for Ottawa, Washington D.C. and then Colorado. It was in the U.S. capital where he had his most productive season—scoring 31 goals and 45 assists in 2002. By 2003, he was in Colorado playing for the Mammoth and had three successful seasons, scoring a total of 65 goals for that franchise through 2005.

"Under league rules, after the end of the year I would have become an unrestricted free-agent, so Colorado did not protect me in the expansion draft," he says. "I was drafted by the Portland Lumberjax. At first, I had really mixed emotions."

However, after meeting with the ownership and the coaching staff of the expansion team, Halladay decided that it would be a great opportunity, signed a contract, and was named a franchise player and team captain.

He immediately made his mark with the team—on January 21, 2006, he scored the winning goal in the franchise's first-ever win. With less than two minutes to play against Colorado at the Rose Garden, Halladay, took a dish from Brodie Merrill and cut towards the net unleashing the winning shot, handing Portland the 12–11 victory.

In 16 games with the Lumberjax in 2006, Halladay scored 18 goals and registered 20 assists in leading the first-year team to the NLL's Western Division title. Nonetheless, the move from Colorado was bittersweet: Halladay was forced to watch the Mammoth win the NLL title in 2006 without him. His former teammates didn't forget him, however.

"Del Halladay taught me more than any other player about the game," remarks former Mammoth teammate Brian Langtry. "He is a master of the pick and roll and moving picks. He cuts really well to the net, and he is a very active shooter. He's also is one of the best at getting open off the ball. I changed my style of play because of Del."

All of the excitement on the lacrosse pitch seems to contradict the relaxed beauty of Canada's wine country. One may not think of Canada as a good growing region for fruit, but Halladay insists the Okanagan Valley is considered a "microregion" and in fact, the southern valley is considered a desert. The area were Elephant Island Orchards resides has warm temperatures and fertile soil, and good sun exposure for growing fruits and berries. "Sometimes the winters can be cold, but it takes a harsh cold spell of minus twenty to thirty degrees before we experience serious frost damage to our crops."

Still, there's the rain. "There can be problems in the winery business from a growing aspect. You can have mold, or mildew, or split cherries from too much rain. One very wet year, we had a cold apricot bloom and lost most of our crop. But we just do our best and learn from our mistakes."

When asked about Halladay's winery/lacrosse combination, Lumberjax Owner/President Angela Batinovich is quick to praise one of her franchise's most important players.

"It's cool he has a lifestyle where he can do something as diverse as playing professional lacrosse and own a winery," she says. "I've been impressed with Del's playing ability. When I invested in the team, he was one of the players I remembered meeting, and we made some phone calls, to arrange a deal for him to come to Portland."

So has the boss tried any of her player's wine?

"As a matter of fact, I have one bottle of his dessert wine in my refrigerator," says Batinovich. "It is very good!"

Bruce Murray

THE FIREFIGHTER

Sports commentators often refer to "heroes" of the game—those athletes who score the winning goal, dish out the winning assist, make the critical stop on defense, disrupt the play and find themselves with the ball at the pivotal moment of the game. Yet true heroes do far more than play sports.

Bruce Murray is one of those people. A firefighter in Vancouver, British Columbia, Murray has revived people with the defibrillator, climbed a fire ladder to pull people out of burning buildings and has been in situations like "flash-overs," when the heat of the fire causes a room to spontaneously combust.

"We usually get there before the ambulance does," says Murray. "Our job is to keep them alive long enough until they can be transported to the hospital. Last night we had two calls for cardiac arrests. One guy made it. One guy didn't."

Those are the days when Murray's job is sobering—and makes his wins and losses as a stand-out defenseman for the NLL's Arizona Sting seem inconsequential. There are no fans, cheerleaders and autographs for Murray when he performs his day-to-day duties in the fire hall. There, Murray is one of six men responsible for a fire truck and a rescue vehicle; the men work alternating four day-and-night alternating shifts. The four days on duty include two ten-hour day shifts and two fourteen-hour night shifts.

"We have a lot to do when we are at the hall waiting for a call," Murray says. In between calls, the firemen run through drills with trucks and ladders, watch instructional videos, cook, clean—and talk around the table.

"Bruce is easy going, rolls with the punches, doesn't say a lot," says Todd Ballard, a fellow firefighter who has worked with the lacrosse star for eight years. "You wouldn't know he was a lacrosse player. He doesn't talk about it much, unless someone asks."

"We watch the games," says Ballard. "Sometimes when there is a skirmish on the field, we tease Bruce about how he picks on the smallest guy. We're like, 'Hey Bruce, you're a big guy"—Murray is 6'1" and 260 pounds—"why don't you fight somebody bigger?'"

Like many aspiring young lacrosse players, Bruce Murray played Junior A Lacrosse in Vancouver until that one fateful day when he was 21 years old and his parents sat him down and asked: What are you going to do with the rest of your life?

"I had always been interested in becoming a firefighter— it goes hand-in-hand with lacrosse," says Murray. "You have to stay in shape, and you have a flexible schedule. There were several firefighters in Vancouver who played in the NLL. The lifestyle looked good to me."

Murray attended the compulsory two years of higher education, fire school and CPR training, and then looked for work.

"I lucked out," he says. "Lots of places were hiring. Although I got rejection letters from eight different departments, I got hired three months after finishing school. It was forty-five minutes from where I grew up."

Murray was drafted by the NLL's Albany Attack in 1998, but he couldn't play for them right away. "The first year as a firefighter, you are on probation," says Murray. "The department doesn't want a rookie doing anything else. You can be fired for using too much sick leave or annual leave. That first year, I had to focus on being a firefighter."

Then, Murray got lucky. When Albany's franchise moved to San Jose, Calif. at the end of the 2003 season, Murray's rights were picked up by the NLL franchise in his hometown of Vancouver.

"I got spoiled playing for Vancouver," he says. "It was near home and my family and friends came to all of the games. It was a great organization."

However, his good fortune didn't last. While Murray established himself as a force in the NLL, the struggling Vancouver Ravens franchise folded at the end of the 2004 season, and his rights were picked-up by Anaheim. After another solid year of play for Murray, the Anaheim team folded, too. Murray was once again on the move, this time to Phoenix, to play for the Arizona Sting, where he brought his play to a new level.

Despite being a "scrapper" defenseman, Murray managed to score three goals—including two critical goals in the playoffs—with seven assists while claiming 77 loose balls in his inaugural season with the Sting.

"It feels good to be involved with a solid organization," Murray says, noting that the Arizona Sting is also associated with, and play in the same arena as, the NHL's Phoenix Coyotes. "I also love sunny Arizona. When people think of Canada they think of snow. It does not snow where I live, but it is rainy for 120 days a year."

What is Murray's favorite away arena in the NLL?

"It has to be playing at Denver," he says. "They have a packed crowd. There is nothing like 18,000 to 19,000 fans booing you to get your juices flowing."

Are there any problems with the travel and being a fire-fighter?

"Well, once or twice there have been problems with flight schedules," he says. "Last year, after an away game at Minnesota, our plane got snowed in. I made a desperate call to one of my buddies to take my shift as there was no way I was going to make it back the next day. Fortunately, he agreed to go in and save my bacon."

Kyle Sweeney

MAKING A LIVING, MAKING A LIFE

Kyle Sweeney is an average New York young entrepreneur, the kind of guy you'd bump into online buying bagels. He's also a star professional athlete—not one of the gossip column regulars who hangs out in trendy nightclubs with rock stars. Sweeney, at 6'2", 190 pounds, is one of the best defensemen in both National League Lacrosse and Major League Lacrosse, a star with both the NLL Philadelphia Wings and the MLL Philadelphia Barrage.

Sweeney's company, in partnership with two other lacrosse insiders, Jay Jalbert and John Gagliardi, is Maverik Lacrosse, a lacrosse clothing and equipment company.

"We are a typical start-up company," says Sweeney. "We have no IT department. In fact, I am the IT department." Sweeney handles accounting, computer programming and logistics, as well as visiting the over sixty retail stores that sell the Maverik line.

"The stores are mostly specialty lacrosse businesses," he says, "and they like to meet us. I enjoy getting out and meeting people, too. It beats staying behind a desk all day."

Sweeney's life in lacrosse began in middle school, in Springfield, Pa. He was looking for something to play other than basketball or football. His father had been a college football player at West Chester University in Pennsylvania and was eager to see Kyle follow in his footsteps; he encouraged Kyle to play lacrosse, thinking of it as a good springtime complement to fall football. Not that Kyle needed his father's lead: his older brother, Brett, already played the game.

"I owe my success to Brett," Sweeney says. "We used to work out in the yard one-on-one. He was the one that got me more committed to the sport, made me quicker, more competitive." Lacrosse became a Sweeney family tradition. Although not turning pro, Brett eventually played varsity lacrosse at Western Maryland College, and younger sister Kerin played on the varsity for Catholic University in Washington, D.C.

As an American in what has historically been a Canadian sport, Sweeney played defense with the "long-pole" in the outdoor high school lacrosse leagues in Springfield.

"Most long-poles don't usually score or help with the offense," he says. "In Springfield, our school was different, which raised a few eyebrows."

In high school, Sweeney did everything with the long-stick. He played long-stick middie (mid-field), took face-offs, played on the man-up squad (power play), and played on the man-down squad.

Not only was Sweeney successful, he became one of the hottest college prospects, as he was named a high school All-American and was called one of the nation's top three long-poles coming out of high school. Soon after the high school championships, the college recruiters came calling with lacrosse scholarships. Sweeney was invited on recruiting trips to perennial college powers such as North Carolina, Virginia and Maryland, but decided on Georgetown University in Washington, D.C.

"I had grown up being a huge Philadelphia Wings fan," he says. "I never thought I could play at that level. I wasn't even sure I could play at the *college* level. So when it came time to choose a college, I chose Georgetown for the academics."

Well, not entirely. He says that Washington, D.C. was a "cool" city, and his coach, Dave Urick, who heads up the Hoya program was an "awesome" coach.

In high school, Sweeney had worn No. 4 as his jersey number, but when he arrived as a freshman on the Hoya team, that number had already been claimed. "I decided to choose No. 7 because that seemed like a cool number. I am kind of superstitious, so I decided if I had a bad year, I would switch numbers for my sophomore year." Sweeney made the team, had a great year, and stuck with his No. 7 throughout his career playing for Georgetown which included two ECAC Defensive Player-of-the-Year awards, as well as being named a three-time All-American. [Kyle still carries his beloved No. 7 as a member of the Philadelphia Wings.]

"My brother Kevin played with Kyle at Georgetown," remarks Colorado's Brian Langtry. "I've never seen anyone take over a game like Kyle Sweeney could in college lacrosse. He's probably the greatest long-stick middie ever to play college lacrosse. He's also one of the few Americans to make the transition to an elite defenseman in the NLL."

Even though his collegiate lacrosse credentials should have assured him a shot at a professional career, upon graduation, Sweeney was once again skeptical.

"I knew I wasn't going to make a ton of money playing lacrosse," he confides, "so I decided to go with security and get a regular job." Sweeney, one to aim high, found a job in finance at Sun Life Financial in New York City. At the same time, he was drafted in the eighth round by the Wings in the 2003 entry draft— a situation that set up a hectic commute.

"Fortunately, I can operate on five or six hours of sleep," Sweeney says.

Sweeney commutes from New York to Philadelphia weekly to the Wednesday night practices. With thirty pounds of lacrosse gear in hand, he stands alongside commuters on the subway to New Jersey. He then meets three Philadelphia Wings teammates who are also commuting from the New York/New Jersey area, and they pile in a car for a two-hour ride from Hoboken, N.J. to Exton, Pa. for the team's 9:30 p.m. practice. After practice, Sweeney has to do the trip in reverse often arriving at his New York City apartment around 3:00 in the morning. If lucky—he gets three hours of sleep before he puts on his suit and heads to the office.

Somehow, he makes it work. He had a solid rookie season with the Wings in 2005, scoring one goal (against the rival Buffalo Bandits) and notching six assists in twelve games. He was even more impressive in his second season, netting four goals and nine assists in fifteen games.

Sweeney's move into NLL lacrosse came with some adjustments—one of the most notable was going from the long-pole (roughly six feet in length) to the typical indoor NLL lacrosse sticks (roughly 3-½ feet in length).

"It is hard to explain for people that do not play lacrosse," he advises, "but it's like taking your favorite golf club that took you years to perfect hitting and then replacing with a golf club half its size, and they still expect you to hit the same way."

Sweeney's favorite moment in lacrosse is the opening face off. "A jail-break," he says. His own assessment of his play: success due to quick hands and aggressive checks. But he says he may not be the best position player on defense—he likes to take chances. Fortunately for Sweeney, this works well for his style of play. He's known as one of the best "take-away" artists in the NLL.

"When I think of Sweeney, I think of how good of a transition player he is," says Rochester's Marshall Abrams. "He has a great set of skills, passing, and vision. I admire how fast he gets up and down the field."

Sweeney says the highlight of the 2006 season was the home victory over the Toronto Rock. "They had beaten us seven times in row," he says. "Not only that, but there was a brotherly rivalry as our coach, Lindsey Sanderson, was the brother of the Toronto coach, Terry Sanderson, and it was in front of our home crowd."

The game was on March 4. Toronto had already beaten Philadelphia earlier in the season 12–11 at Toronto. This time the Wings got their revenge. Although Philadelphia trailed 9–5 at the half, it was Sweeney who scored the first goal of the third period—an unassisted goal that brought his team within three. This sparked a 6–1 domination of the third period, which the Wings went on to win 14–12 in front of a raucous crowd at Wachovia Center in Philadelphia.

Sweeney can also add another moment to his illustrious professional lacrosse career—champion. Sweeney was a member of the Philadelphia Barrage MLL team that pummeled the Denver Outlaws 23–12 in front of 5,374 fans at the Home Depot Center in Carson, California, to win the championship (Steinfeld Cup) in 2006.

"He's a great all-around player," comments MLL teammate Armando Polanco. "He's got a great stick, he's super fast, and he virtually never gets beaten on defense. In the outdoor league, he wasn't beaten once all season. This never happens. Because of his speed, nobody beats Kyle Sweeney. Kyle is a hustler, scrambles for loose balls, he'll scrap, he'll fight, and he'll do anything to win. He's also a nice guy off the field."

Sweeney, who loves to travel, aspires to be a globe trotter and help spread the gospel of lacrosse in new countries. "My dream job," he says, "would be to start lacrosse programs in Ireland."

Armando Polanco

WORKING AND PLAYING
IN TIMES SQUARE

Like all New Yorkers and many people around the world, lacrosse standout Armando Polanco vividly remembers the morning of September 11, 2001.

"I was just getting into work and stopped to talk with the receptionist," Polanco says. "She was watching a television and she said a small airplane had hit one of the World Trade towers. I watched the screen and then all-of-a-sudden, on live television, another airplane crashed into the second tower. My first comment was: 'That wasn't a small plane.'"

Polanco, a marketing director for MTV in Manhattan and, at the time, a member of the NLL's New York Saints, watched the scenes unfold with his horrified co-workers. "Our office is in Times Square. We thought we could be a target. Everyone I talked to said we had to get out of the city."

Polanco left work, hoping to be able to get home to Long Island. He briskly walked down to Penn Station to catch a train, but upon arriving, learned that all transportation has been stopped. He could not reach any members of his family on his cell phone. Service was down. Along with thousands of other New Yorkers, he walked to the 59th Street bridge to cross over to the borough of Queens. There, he was able to reach his mother on the cell phone.

"She was crying, telling me to get out of the city. She was watching the news, all the people covered in soot. She didn't realize I wasn't that close to the Trade Towers. Then, I was able to reach my dad." Polanco's father, who works in the construction industry and has assignments working all over the city, just happened to be working in Queens that day. Against all odds, considering the congestion of pedestrians and that no traffic was moving, Polanco found his father, hopped in his truck, and made it home.

In the days that followed, as the initial shock wore off, Polanco, like thousands of other New Yorkers, made the priority to get the city, business, and life back to normal. Part of "normal" in America is the resumption of sporting events, including the NLL season in New York. After a brief discussion, it was obvious that the 2002 professional lacrosse season would go on as planned for the Polanco's team, the New York Saints.

If you had to pick one word to describe Polanco's lacrosse career it would be "patience." After growing up in Oceanside, N.Y., and attending Nassau Community College, Polanco's lacrosse career blossomed at nearby Hofstra University.

"I was a good player, but not an All-American," he says, "I was all-conference and wanted to succeed at the highest level at whatever I did. I wanted to play professional lacrosse."

However, after he graduated 1999 and waited through the news reports of the late rounds of the NLL draft, he learned that he was not drafted.

"I was very disappointed," he says. "I tried to make the best of it. Lacrosse had been good to me. I got a scholarship to play for Hofstra, so it helped get me through school. I was disappointed that it had to end."

So Polanco went to work—as a marketing exec at MTV ("No, I don't make music videos." he says.)

"I had a non-paying internship my senior year at Hofstra," he says. "It was supposed to be for a half a year, but they liked me so much, they extended it for a full year."

This internship got his foot in the door, but it was lacrosse that tipped the scales in his favor over other well-qualified applicants.

"The guy who was hiring had done his graduate work at Hofstra and seen some lacrosse games," says Polanco. "He didn't know who I was then, but the fact that I played varsity sports was a positive. He liked the competitive drive and teamwork that sports demand."

"I was still trying to play a little lacrosse. Hofstra had a club that included students who had graduated. I played in some local clubs and a few tournaments. I didn't want to give it up. Then, I got the phone call that changed everything."

The call was from a former Hofstra teammate, Brian Spallina, who played lacrosse for the Saints. Before the 2002 season, the coach of the Saints wanted to have an open try-out for non-drafted players in the New York area to supplement the talent of the drafted players. Not only did Polanco answer the call, he made the team.

Polanco, however, had one small problem: he had not yet told his boss at MTV that he was going to be moonlighting as a professional lacrosse player.

"Luckily, my boss was very supportive," he says. "I had to sacrifice all my vacation time, and it was difficult driving the hour for the Wednesday practices at the indoor facility at Mt. Sinai in Suffolk County, Long Island, but it was worth it."

Polanco knew he was only going to be a part-time player —he appeared in eight games, or roughly half of the games his first season in 2002. However, he can still remember the call he received from Saints Coach Sal LoCascio, the night before the Saints game against the Columbus Landsharks, telling him he would be suiting up for his first game.

"I was nervous," he recalls. "I worked half-a-day on Friday. I went straight from work to LaGuardia and caught a plane to Columbus for the game. I was still in my work clothes."

"I've suited up in lots of different locker rooms, but this one was beautiful," he says. "It was the visiting locker room for the National Hockey League's Columbus Blue Jackets."

In professional lacrosse, because many players come directly from a "day job," they take showers *before* the games.

"After I came out of the shower, someone had draped the jerseys over the lockers, and it hit me. I'd made it. I was going to play professional lacrosse."

"During the game, I was so pumped up I was jumping on the bench," he says. "As soon as I saw action, I hit someone. I was so fired up, I checked this guy completely to the floor. After that first hit, I settled down, wasn't nervous anymore, and focused on playing my game. I remember some scraps in the corner, and I remember how much fun it was."

In Polanco's second year with the Saints in 2003, he experienced his first fight. The 2003 season was difficult for Polanco and the rest of the Saints—there was a lot of tension as the owners were having trouble making payroll—and it was becoming more and more obvious that the team might fold after the season.

"The coach was great, but the management was a mess that season," Polanco reflects. "It was the players who kept that team together."

The Saints were on a difficult road trip that saw them fly to the West Coast and lose a tough game to Vancouver, and then fly back half way across Canada—in the middle of a blizzard—to play in Calgary. During that game, the Roughnecks were on a fast break when Polanco charged out of the box to catch the ball carrier. It came down to a foot race.

"I was trying to give him a legal check on the side," he recalls. "I was late, and checked him on the back." The Calgary player, Shawn Cable, flew into the boards head first and crumpled.

Scott Forbes, the 6'2", 235-pound Calgary enforcer and, as bad luck would have it, Cable's best friend on the team, sprang into action.

"His gloves were off and he shoved my mask off," Polanco says. "I knew I had to fight. I got my gloves off as fast as I could and started swinging. It felt like the fight lasted fifteen minutes, but it was probably over in thirty seconds. He kept throwing punches. I threw punches. At some point I got his mask off. I remember landing some good shots, and he certainly landed some good shots on me. At one point I tried to throw him into the boards, but he grabbed my jersey and we both ended up hitting the boards, and fell down together. We wrestled on the ground trying to throw punches until the refs stopped the fight."

The fight fired up his team, with his teammates telling him "good scrap," as he went to the penalty box.

"I'm glad that I earned respect from my teammates as well as the team from Calgary," he says. "Some of the Canadians think Americans are a little soft. I gave as good as I got."

What was more interesting was what happened after the game. The blizzard that engulfed Calgary limited the options for air flights, as well as celebrations after the game. The Saints found a bar after the game and sure, enough, some of the Roughnecks were already there.

"I was sitting at the bar with my brother Nicky," Armando recalls, "and I kept seeing this guy looking over at me. Whenever I looked up it was like he was staring at me. Then it dawned on me. That was the guy I had the fight with."

Due to the masks and pads it sometimes takes lacrosse players a moment to recognize each other in street clothes, but they inevitably do. Suddenly, Forbes, the Calgary player, stood up and walked over to Polanco. Polanco turned to his brother and said, "Are you kidding me? This guy wants to fight again."

Polanco took his watch off, and handed it to his brother and told Nicky to watch his stuff as he prepared for another face-off.

"Before Scott Forbes reached me, he stopped at the bar, got two beers. Then, he comes up and hands me one. He says, 'Hey, good scrap. Why don't you say we leave it on the field?'"

But that's not the end of the story. The teams met again that season in New York. There were no fisticuffs on the field, and Polanco ended up taking his new friends from Calgary-Forbes and Cable—to the MTV studios for a tour.

"Other than the guys on my team, they've turned out to be my best friends in the league," he says.

Unfortunately for Polanco, he lost his weekend job in 2003, when the Saints ceased operations.

"It was a shame," Polanco says. "Management didn't treat us well, but we had good players, like All-Star goalie Gee Nash, and Gavin Prout who is probably the best player I ever played with. I thought about re-locating, but I work for MTV (MTV has roughly 20,000 partnerships with local cable companies around the country, often owned by Time/Warner, Comcast, or Cox Cable and Polanco puts together the national marketing plan to get these cable providers to pick up new stations, and sell local advertising). Neither the office in Los Angeles or Chicago is close to a lacrosse team."

"Everybody loves Armando," says his supervisor, Stephanie Ruyle who has worked with him for eight years. "He is a great collaborator, a great team-player. Part of Armando's job is to make sure MTV has a presence at trade shows—like trade shows in the electronics industry or the wireless industry. Armando is great at representing the company, and level-headed when it comes to solving unexpected problems. When meeting with the sales team or being at one of these trade events, there is always some unexpected request. Armando is great at handling the situation and working with the clients to get them what they want. He really shows good judgment on the fly."

Although he was no longer a member of a professional lacrosse team, in 2003, Polanco had another high-profile playing opportunity. That year, the World Lacrosse Championships were held in Guelph, Canada and, because of contract and scheduling disputes associated with Major League Lacrosse, many of the world's best players were not permitted to play. Since he was out of professional lacrosse at the time, Polanco accepted an invitation to represent the United States.

"We got some expenses reimbursed, but I knew the trip would cost money," he says. "I had to take off a week from work to live in the dorms in Canada that had no television. In some respects we were considered the "B" team because some of our best players couldn't play, but I would never trade anything for the experience of representing my country. I now have a USA jersey with my name on it. It would have been nice to win"—Canada beat the Iroquois Nation for gold; the US defeated Scotland for the bronze—"but it was great just to be there."

From 2004 to the summer of 2006, Polanco stayed in good physical condition playing club lacrosse in Long Island and kept involved in the pros by watching brother Nicky Polanco play for the MLL's Long Island Lizards. By the summer of 2006, Armando played a few outdoor games for the MLL's Philadelphia Barrage with Ryan Boyle and Kyle Sweeney.

Still, Polanco knew his best opportunity for play pro indoor lacrosse would come only if the game returned to New York City. In 2006, this became reality with the announcement that New York City would receive an expansion NLL franchise—the New York Titans—starting with the 2007 season.

"Every year, we'd hear rumors that a new franchise was starting, that some owner was moving to New York, but every time it turned out not to be true," says Polanco. "It wasn't until I got a call from Coach Adam Mueller in the summer of 2006 that I believed it. He said he was the coach, he had a good system that needs athletic Americans like me and Nicky, and he wanted us to play. It's exciting."

While Polanco was one of the Titans' initial signed players, he was cut from the squad just a month before the start of the Titans season.

A loss for lacrosse, but a gain for MTV.

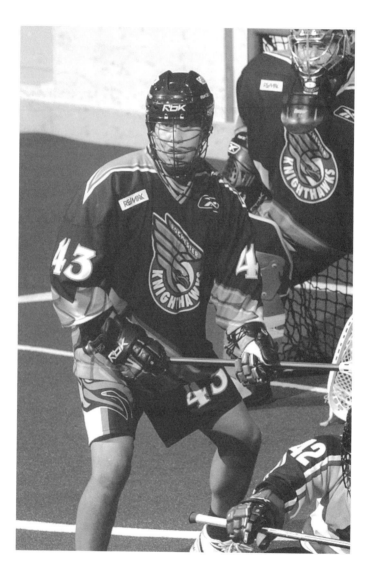

Marshall Abrams

A NATIVE AMERICAN PLAYS THE NATIVE SPORT

The prowess of North America's Native Americans in the game they developed as "baggataway" centuries ago is not just an item for the history books. Approximately six percent of today's professional lacrosse players are Native Americans, including one of the sport's best athletes, Marshall Abrams, a member of the Iroquois Onondaga Nation. Abrams, a star defenseman for both the NLL's Rochester Knighthawks and the MLL's Rochester Rattlers, is also financial manager at Mass Mutual insurance, and husband to Cheri, and father to son Maccoy and daughter Grace. His children attend elementary school on the Onondaga Nation, five miles south of Syracuse, N.Y., as Abrams is raising his family as he was raised, schooling them in the customs and traditions of one of the tribes of the Iroquois Nation.

Balancing lacrosse and a job and a family and school hasn't been easy, particularly from a geographically limited area of upstate New York.

"When I first started playing in the NLL," Abrams says, "I was drafted by the Columbus Landsharks in Ohio and I went there to play. It was hectic. At the same time, I was majoring in biology—a difficult major—at Syracuse—a difficult school. I was in my fifth year, getting a degree, and I also worked in a pharmaceutical lab, second shift, doing quality control. I barely saw my wife and my newborn child, and there came a point when I didn't feel it was worth it to be playing lacrosse."

Yet that was not the only hardship Abrams endured balancing work, school, and lacrosse his first year in the NLL. "It was the strangest thing—because of how the flights work, it seemed to take me eight hours to get to Columbus no matter what I did. If I took a flight—due to layovers and flight schedules—it took me eight hours to fly from Syracuse to Columbus. If I drove—it also took me eight hours. For home games, I usually wouldn't be home by three in the morning. After the first year, in 2001, I asked the Landsharks to please trade me—due to my family situation—and they obliged."

Thus, in the 2002 season, Abrams began his career with the Rochester Knighthawks—"just" eighty-six miles from his home.

The move to Rochester reunited Abrams with his old high school assistant coach, Regy Thorpe, a veteran with the Knighthawks. It was during this time frame that he found himself between jobs.

"Regy told me they were hiring guys at Mass Mutual, and recommended that I submit an application," says Abrams. "He said that hiring a Native American would also be seen as a positive by the company."

He was hired. His first boss was Wayne Lafluer, a childhood friend of Regy Thorpe. "The financial industry is a complex and grueling choice and as a manager, finding a qualified individual that can overcome those aspects can be an arduous task," says Lafluer. "Marshall transferred his work ethic from the lacrosse field into the boardroom. His integrity and character are a perfect fit for a broad spectrum of clients and assure him a successful career."

A career in the insurance industry seems to perfectly suit Abrams and his moonlighting activities as a professional lacrosse star.

"It works out great with my schedule," Abrams says. "I work on commission basis, meaning I only make money if I complete the insurance deals. So, in some respects, if I don't work, I don't get paid. It's up to me to put in the effort that I need to make a living."

For Abrams, the journey to his athletic career began when he was very young, learning his Native American culture.

"If you go on the reservation, you won't immediately notice much difference, but what is different is the people," he says. "Everyone knows each other - some have lived there for generations. It is a very tight-knit community. The community cares very much about preserving its songs, language, traditions. And one of those traditions is lacrosse."

Abrams was given his first lacrosse stick at age three, and he began playing organized lacrosse—as organized as it can be —at age four.

"All of my ancestors played," he says. "Both of my grandfathers played. It was the natural thing to do in our community."

After eighth grade, he transferred to Lafayette High School, a school not in the Onondaga Nation. Lafayette was his first experience in an integrated school and his prodigious lacrosse talent helped him fit right in. At Lafayette, he played varsity lacrosse. One of his volunteer assistant coaches was Thorpe, who in addition to playing professionally for Rochester, was a member of Syracuse's 1993 NCAA championship lacrosse team.

"Regy was playing professional at that point," Abrams says about his high school days, "but what we kids were impressed with is that he'd played for Syracuse team. Syracuse is right up the road—and lots of us kids hoped to play college lacrosse for the Orangemen."

In high school, Abrams switched from playing forward to playing defense. "Regy must have had something to do with it," he says. "Maybe put a bug in my ear. I can't remember why I switched."

Although he was All-County his senior year at Lafayette, he was not actively recruited by any college—but he had scouts in his corner.

"Both Regy and the Lafayette coach, Friedman Bucktooth, knew the Syracuse coaches, and they told the coaches I could play," says Abrams. "I received a four-year lacrosse scholarship pretty much based on their recommendations. They also pushed me to get good grades and to make the application to Syracuse. Two weeks before classes started, I learned I'd been accepted."

Abrams' days at Syracuse were eventful. The Orangemen continued their national lacrosse prominence. After the 1999 team lost to Virginia 12–10 in the NCAA finals, the 2000 team, when Abrams was a senior, went to the NCAA Championships on a mission: No Syracuse seniors had left the university without a championship ring since 1987. Abrams and the Orangeman did not disappoint. Syracuse overpowered Princeton 13–7, and won another NCAA title.

Upon graduating, Abrams began his professional lacrosse career with the MLL outdoor league, touring the northeast part of the United States in exhibition games to promote the league. "I loved it," he says. "We visited Boston, New York, Philadelphia, Ohio. It was great."

Within weeks of the tour, Abrams was a first-round draft selection of the NLL's Columbus Landsharks.

"Like I said, it was tough playing for Columbus because of the travel schedule, but it was great to play with a bunch of young guys," he says. "It wasn't a great team, but there were lots of future stars in the league who played there."

A vivid memory for Abrams is his first NLL game, when Columbus played an away game against the New York Saints at the Nassau Coliseum in Uniondale, N.Y. "Our team was leading. It was in the middle of the game, and there was a tripping penalty that was pretty rough. People took exception, and kept jawing and shoving, and then it escalated into a line-brawl. It wasn't a bench-brawl. Everyone on the field got into it."

When the smoke cleared, Abrams, the rookie defenseman, was one of five Landshark players who were ejected from the game.

"It was an away game and we'd only suited up fifteen players. Suddenly, we were down to ten players for the rest of the game, and the Saints had more players in uniform. They wore us down, and we lost."

As a Knighthawk, Abrams has made a significant impact. In his first season with Rochester in 2002, he scored five goals and dished out 15 assists. This was followed by a solid 2003 season in which he played in all sixteen games, added one goal, four assists, and, in a memorable night in Albany, collected his 200th career loose ball.

Unfortunately, in 2004, Abrams suffered a season-ending injury at an away game in Philadelphia; as a result, he saw limited action in 2005.

"I have seen him play and he makes it look easy," says Lafluer, also a lacrosse aficionado. "Offensive opponents are well aware of Marshall's abilities and usually look for alternative routes to the cage. His intimidation factor is a result of his consistent and solid game play. There is nothing scarier than a warrior who is fierce and smart."

Still, Abrams has a few regrets. "There is one thing that still bugs me," he says. "The 2003 Championship Game against Toronto."

This was not an ordinary night for the Abrams family. His wife was pregnant and expecting their second child the night of the championship game. Abrams stayed by her side in the birthing center until the last possible moment—six o'clock. He kissed Cheri goodbye, drove to Rochester to play—and his daughter, Grace, was born fifteen minutes later.

But, wait, that's not the regret.

"I made it to Rochester on-time, got dressed, and was ready at the start of the game," Abrams says. "It was during the Toronto dynasty of three straight championships. They were definitely favored, but I thought we had a better team." Rochester had tied Buffalo for the best record in the league—12–4. Yet, it was the 11–5 Toronto Rock that was victorious that night. The Rochester team that had scored 16 goals to win the semifinal game against Buffalo could only manage six goals against the stingy Rock defense and Champions Cup MVP Bob Watson, the Rock goalie.

"It still bugs me," Abrams repeats. "We had a better team, but they had a hot goalie. It was a missed opportunity—the best opportunity we had to win the championship."

Ryan Boyle

THE FASTEST SPORT IN THE
FASTEST CITY

The whistle blew to stop play during a pre-season scrimmage between the San Jose Stealth and the Arizona Sting and the Stealth's second-overall draft pick, Ryan Boyle, cradled the ball behind the net. Despite the stoppage, Ryan nonchalantly waltzed into the crease and let a shot rip as others stood around. The ball missed its target, clanging off the Arizona goalie's mask. During the line-change, an enforcer from the Sting put the rookie in a headlock, escorted him to the bench, and threatened bodily harm if Boyle pulled another stunt like that. That was lacrosse-speak for "Welcome to the pros, rookie." Boyle learned fast: in 2005, he was the NLL Rookie of the Year.

Now, Boyle is one of the poster boys for New York City's new franchise, the Titans. Or, as he says, "I play the fastest sport in the fastest city."

Boyle's memorable first scrimmage was not the first time the slashing attacker has been roughed up on the playing field—it began at the hands of his older brothers. When he was four, he cried when he was not allowed to go to lacrosse practice with his brother, Patrick; his mother finally agreed. It was doubtful that Boyle, many years from growing into his adult frame of 5'11", 180 pounds, could do much with a lacrosse stick as a preschooler. But he did begin a lifetime love affair with the game.

Boyle draws strength from the years he played youth league lacrosse—experience that he now passes down through Trilogy Lacrosse, a company he formed with a former Princeton teammate Rob Lindsey.

"I get to chase my dream," he says. "Not only that, how many people can say they love their job? I do." Boyle calls himself a "nomad" for his traveling lifestyle. One month during the fall, Trilogy Lacrosse—which is based in Boyle's current home of Austin, Texas—took him to lacrosse camps in New Jersey, Nashville, Lexington, Kentucky, Houston and Seattle; he also found the time to play in a tournament in Hawaii.

In Austin, what started as a consulting gig to train high school kids, draw-up plays, establish lacrosse drills and establish realistic practice schedules for high school students, has morphed into something much larger. Boyle and Trilogy have set up youth programs in the community to develop talent at younger ages and act as a feeder program into varsity and junior varsity teams.

"I love working with younger kids," says Boyle. "They are so intense and in this day of political correctness, bluntly honest, which is refreshing." Boyle also likes to keep the fun in the game and encourages young kids to develop their own celebratory dance after each goal. He's also learned to be careful about what he says.

Once, when the kids in the camp asked Boyle what position they should play he said, "Attackers—you get to score goals, celebrate, and pick up chicks."

Soon after the practice ended, one of the player's moms asked her ten-year-old what he'd learned that day. The young player repeated Boyle's words verbatim. The mom had a good sense of humor, but Boyle heard about it, nonetheless. It was an important lesson.

When Boyle was drafted by the San Jose Stealth, he'd never been out west, had never played "box" or indoor lacrosse, and was not used to seeing his teammates (many of whom fly in from all over the country, and Canada) only once a week for games. "It is a lot rougher, with off-ball checking, quick line changes. A player takes an incessant beating out there," he says.

Boyle is the first to admit he is superstitious. Beginning in high school, Boyle would listen to specific music, in a specific order, eat at the same restaurant, dress in the same order —and "freaked out" if something interfered with his routine. Maturity has lessened his reliance on his eccentricities, but he frequently imposes his appalling fashion sense on his teammates, with his "lucky pants"—blue, bellbottom trousers with shamrocks.

And then, there's his "lucky number"—14. Like many players in the NLL, Boyle was a multi-star athlete in high school. He played quarterback for The Gilman School Greyhounds junior varsity football team as No. 14, where the *Baltimore Sun* named him twice All-Metro and where he led his team to two "A" conference titles after a 21-game winning streak.

In the winter, when Boyle played point guard for the high school basketball team, he fed once again on good karma and chose No. 14—and his team tied for the division championship.

By the time springtime came around, and with it, lacrosse, Boyle insisted on No. 14. It worked. *The Sun* named him "Player of the Year," after he scored 36 goals and 44 assists (his high school career final numbers were 131 goals and 127 assists). In 2000, *The Sun* claimed that not only the Princeton-bound Boyle was the best player in Maryland, but there was "perhaps no better senior in the nation."

When Boyle made the varsity team at Princeton, he figured that as a freshman, he'd have to switch numbers, that he'd get the last pick—but happily, No. 14 was available. And so, when he was drafted by the San Jose Stealth, his first request was be no surprise: "Could I please have No. 14?"

The Stealth drafted Boyle right out of Princeton in 2004 and the Baltimore boy moved to California. There, he collected 22 goals, 42 assists and found 95 loose balls during his rookie season.

Boyle's typical weekly schedule starts with a de-toxing on Monday—recovering not just from the brutal, bruising play of the weekend, but from the jet lag as well. By Tuesday, he's back at work, at Trilogy, writing and arranging material for his upcoming lacrosse camps, marketing and promoting his camps, talking with his business partner, and of course, promoting lacrosse, which sometimes includes "coaching the coaches."

Boyle loves to develop programs where there are coaches and players with a ton of enthusiasm, but not necessarily a ton of lacrosse knowledge. He arranges offensive sets and arranges and oversees skills training of the players, which can include dodging, passing and stick. Boyle's job with Trilogy does come in handy as it allows him to work on his shooting and passing and to "play lacrosse while I'm not playing lacrosse."

Surprisingly, Boyle does not think it hurts his team's performance not to play together every day. "It does put a lot of pressure on you at training camp," he says, as this is the one time of year teammates have lengthy periods to work on plays. "But in indoor lacrosse you can't do plays that are too intricate as the action is so fast and the defense will snuff it out.

The San Jose franchise struggled during the 2005–2006 indoor season, and while Boyle says he "hates to lose," there were plenty of highlights for the second-year player. One was the season's opener—which the Stealth won in a thrilling overtime—and in which three OCC choppers and a monster truck opened the game in a circus-like atmosphere on the home field of the expansion Edmonton Rush.

A few weeks later, Boyle and his teammates met and tossed around a lacrosse ball with National Hockey League Hall-of-Fame player Wayne Gretzky, whose NHL's Phoenix Coyotes were in town to play the San Jose Sharks. Like many Canadian youngsters, Gretzky had played lacrosse as a child, and after being handed a stick, played a bit of catch with Boyle and some fellow Stealth players.

In only two years as a professional lacrosse player, Boyle has already gained respect from his teammates and competitors.

Philadelphia Barrage teammate Armando Polanco says, "Ryan is the smartest lacrosse player I've ever met. He knows every aspect of the game. He is like the coach on the field. And he also acts like a coach off the field—talking lacrosse and sharing his knowledge. Ryan is the Peyton Manning of lacrosse. He makes everyone on his team better. I've never seen anyone better at getting the ball to the net and in the net. He flat out knows how to analyze and beat defenses."

Marshall Abrams of the Rochester Knighthawks observes, "Ryan is a quick and fast player. He's not the biggest guy in the league, but he's so quick and he has great passing and great vision. He can split on a dime—totally change directions. Playing defense, he is one of the hardest guys to keep track of."

Yet despite his Princeton education, the attention of being a professional lacrosse player, and the exponential growth of his company, Boyle is modest.

"I'm a wanderer," he says. "I'll go where life takes me."

Brian Langtry

THE TEACHER WITH THE BLACK EYE

A forward for both of Colorado's professional lacrosse teams, Brian Langtry excels in a sport where fights are commonplace, the action is rough and bumps, bruises, and black eyes suffered on the weekend are often still visible on Monday morning. For Langtry, Monday morning means standing in front of seventh and eighth graders at the Challenge School in the Cherry Creek School District near Denver. Langtry, who has a master's in teaching from Dowling College in Oakdale, N.Y., says, "Yeah, I guess in one way a teacher isn't acting as a role-model by fighting, but nobody has ever mentioned anything like that to me. And if they did, I would tell them, it's part of the game."

Langtry grew up on Long Island, in Massapequa, N.Y., started playing lacrosse when he was "seven or eight," and by high school was an outstanding player for St. Anthony's High School, a perennial top lacrosse team on Long Island. And in the fall, he played football.

"By my junior year, I was the starting quarterback," he says. "I'm not going to be modest. I would say I was the best player on the team. Then, during a game, I went down in a rough tackle between players and my leg snapped in two."

Langtry, now 5'10", 185 pounds, still has a metal rod in his leg.

The spring of his junior year—the time when colleges do their heaviest recruiting for athletic scholarships—his leg was barely healed—but he still played lacrosse.

"The first day of lacrosse practice was the first day I could run again after my injury," he says. "I ended up scoring 25 points my junior year, but my mobility was severely limited."

His efforts were good enough—he received letters of interest from Syracuse, Johns Hopkins, Brown and North Carolina. However, he was most heavily recruited by local Hofstra University.

"At the time, I had a girlfriend in the area, and my older brother Rich was playing lacrosse for Hofstra"—Rich would later play pro briefly with the then-Bridgeport Barrage of the MLL—"so, I decided staying close to home was the best thing for me."

Brian returned to true form his senior year at St. Anthony's and scored an outrageous 70 goals and 30 assists in only a fifteen-game season. Yet, unlike other pro players, who had glory days in college lacrosse, Langtry reflects differently on his stint at Hofstra.

"Although I enjoyed playing with my brother, I didn't enjoy the whole experience," he says. "Hofstra ran a very set offense. It was a limited system with passing and ball control. There wasn't much of an opportunity for me to do ball handling or be creative. It was frustrating, and maybe my ego got in the way as well. We were ranked as high as No. 4 in the country my junior year, but looking back, I would have fit better into a Syracuse-style system."

These are interesting comments for a guy who was an All-American, the American East "Player-of-the-Year," and the third-leading scorer in the nation his senior year. Professional scouts were impressed. Langtry was drafted thirty-eighth by the New York Saints. Although he may have been on a "high" to be drafted by a professional team, he wasn't in a good situation: he did not officially make the team and was relegated to the practice squads in '98 and '99.

"It was terrible," he says. "I lived on Long Island and I had to commute over an hour-and-a-half to the Bronx to practice. The team was terrible. There was constant turnover. I'll admit I didn't put in one hundred percent."

He did have one memorable experience in his short career with the Saints (he was to play only three career games, all in 2000). It was during a home game against the Buffalo Bandits when he scored his first NLL goal, but it was memorable for something else.

"I was pumped," he says. "I was being a bit of a jack-ass. I talk too much anyway. I was in a face-off against Andy Ogilvie"—most recently with the Calgary Roughnecks—"and I didn't know who he was. I took a baseball-like swing at his neck, and we dropped the gloves and started fighting."

Langtry should have done his homework. Not only was he outmatched on paper—Ogilvie is 6'1" and weighs 210 pounds—but he's considered one of the toughest guys ever to play in the NLL.

"I remember some punches and then Ogilvie picked me up and dropped me on my head," says Langtry with a laugh. "My parents had come to watch the game. So, basically, I got beat up in front of my parents."

Langtry received five penalty minutes for the fight with Ogilvie, but more importantly, the game marked the end of his career with the Saints. He had appeared in three games, scored the one goal, and collected six loose balls. In 2001, while on the practice squad, he got the letter—he'd been cut.

"I'm still bitter at that," he says. "They didn't call me or anything. They just sent me a letter in the mail."

Langtry was out of the NLL, but he stayed active in lacrosse, working as an assistant coach at Dowling College while receiving his Masters in Teaching. He also played MLL lacrosse —eventually playing for the Bridgeport Barrage, the Baltimore Bayhawks and the Denver Outlaws. During that time, he and his wife, Missy, moved to Colorado (the family now includes daughter Lucy and son Magnus).

In 2003, there were rumors that Colorado would be getting a National Lacrosse League franchise. Langtry began to consider making a comeback into NLL lacrosse.

"I figured Colorado couldn't have an indoor team without me on it," he says. He had a contact with the new franchise, general manager Steve Govett, who arranged for Brian to attend the team try-out. However, he couldn't make the try-out, so he went to the mass try-out instead—one that was open to anyone in the Denver area.

"I dominated the try-outs," he says. "Some of these guys had been just adult league players, hadn't even played college ball. Some guys couldn't throw or catch."

At first, a few members of the coaching staff thought Langtry might be too small—but they decided to take a chance. His first break came in an exhibition game against the Toronto Rock in 2003, when he scored the game-winning goal in overtime. In the next game he played, against Philadelphia in front of 12,000 fans that had stayed in the arena following a Colorado Avalanche National Hockey League game, Langtry rose to the occasion, scoring four goals and registering two assists.

Once again, he was on top of the lacrosse world.

The Mammoth front office had learned that Langtry's brief experience with New York in 2000 did not count as a full season, so he was considered a rookie for the 2003 season. After winning NLL Rookie of the Week honors several times over, he was named the 2003 NLL Rookie of the Year. He'd garnered 28 goals and 34 assists.

Although he calls 2004, his sophomore year, "crappy," he still managed 24 goals and 26 assists in 16 games. Then, in 2005, he was benched for the first few games of the season. "The team had picked up a lot of right-handed veteran forwards," he says. "Finally, several parents and students from the Challenge School called the Mammoth front office and begged them to let me play. I don't know if that influenced the front office or not, but it sure was nice of those kids. And that coach got fired."

By 2006, the new coach was the legendary Gary Gait.

"I knew Gary knew I was capable," he says. "I knew I could be successful and be an All-Star." He was. And along the way, Langtry scored 24 goals, registered 26 assists, and helped lead the Colorado Mammoth to the 2006 NLL Championship.

In his "other life," Langtry is not only considered an outstanding teacher, he is the Johnny Appleseed of lacrosse in his school district.

"When I first came here there were maybe five kids who played lacrosse—now there are 55," he says. "Not only that, but there are probably fifty families who hold Mammoth season tickets."

"Brian's greatest attribute is his fierceness," teammate Gavin Prout says. "He is not afraid of anything. He's not afraid to miss a goal. In overtime, sometimes players get tentative because nobody wants to screw up and lose the game. Not Brian. He's a gambler. He'll take the shot, and often he *doesn't* miss— that's why he has so many game-winning goals."

"And he's a character, he's nuts," Dan Carey, another teammate, adds. "Brian is so full of energy, he gets so hyped in the locker room."

"He is a character," Prout agrees, "He jokes, he pulls pranks in the locker room—he's the type of guy every team needs. I remember a couple of times, Gary Gait would be giving a serious speech before a game and everyone is quiet when he finishes. Then Langtry says some off-the-wall comment, everybody's laughing, wondering what planet he's from."

Sounds like the junior-high-school teacher has picked up a few antics from his students.

Chris McKay

LIVING EVERY CANADIAN
KID'S DREAM

At first glance, he could be any twenty-something college graduate aspiring to be a firefighter in Victoria, British Columbia. He is athletic, has already attended fire college outside Dallas, Texas and he is certified to perform CPR. Like many aspiring firefighters, he holds down part-time jobs until he becomes selected to be a full-fledged fire fighter.

However, Chris McKay's part-time job is not typical of any firefighter. When not showing bravery and fortitude in saving lives as one of Vancouver's finest, McKay is a star defenseman with the National Lacrosse League's Arizona Sting.

"It's every Canadian kids dream to play professional lacrosse," says McKay.

With his prodigious talent, it is not surprising McKay found his way into professional lacrosse, but he had a few twists and turns in the road before he got there. He earned three varsity letters and became the captain of his lacrosse team at Mt. Douglas High School in Victoria and took recruiting trips to schools as far away as New York. On his way back from a trip to the east coast, he visited a friend in Indianapolis, Indiana who happened to know the coach for the Butler University lacrosse team. Sure enough, the coach liked what he heard and saw from the young Canadian player, and after McKay returned home, he got a phone call from the coach offering him a lacrosse scholarship.

At this point McKay had to make a decision. He had been invited to the Toronto Rock training camp, and had made the roster, but would not be regularly suiting up. He had to weigh this opportunity of playing in the NLL with playing in college. "Butler was a Division I school, and offered a good education, and a beautiful campus," he says. "I had to take it." It also gave him an opportunity to travel up and down the eastern seaboard and see places he would not normally have seen as a Canadian citizen. At Butler, McKay played long-stick midfielder for the Bulldogs, and was named team captain his senior year. Combined with his outstanding performance with the Victoria Junior A squad, it was not surprising the NLL called again after graduation.

McKay' s ambitions were realized when he was drafted by the nearby Vancouver Ravens franchise in the first round, the seventh pick overall in the 2004 NLL entry draft.

There was only one problem. The team folded. In no time, he was drafted in the dispersal draft by the Rochester Knight-hawks. "I just couldn't see moving three time zones away and living in New York for the league minimum salary of $6,000 a year. I told them, sorry, I just couldn't do it."

His professional career, however, was saved by the bell—or rather—the Sting. In a move that allowed McKay to continue to play in the NLL, he was traded to the Arizona Sting.

"I had already missed two games of the season when the Arizona general manager called me and asked me to play for them," he says. "It was closer to home and I decided to give it a try. I was eager to play."

Despite being on the back-line, McKay, a star defenseman, scored four goals and registered eight assists in 13 games as a rookie in 2005. Although the team ended the regular season with a mediocre 9–7 record, the Sting had a Cinderella run to the NLL Championship Game, upsetting both the Colorado Mammoth and the Calgary Roughnecks on the way. Against Colorado, the Sting erased a 7–3 first period deficit to beat the Mammoth 16–13 in the first round. Against Calgary in the semifinals, Arizona trailed 11–7 in the third period, but rallied to win the game 19–15.

In the wings, awaiting the championship game was the Toronto Rock—the team with the NLL's best regular season record at 12–4, and a team that was appearing in the final game for the fifth time in six years.

"Toronto is the Mecca of lacrosse. There were 19,500 fans in the stands," says McKay. "Toronto and Colorado are my two favorite places to play on the road because the fans are so into lacrosse." The fans in Toronto had plenty to cheer about that night: the Rock downed the upstart Sting 19–13 for the crown.

During his rookie year in 2005, McKay lived full-time in Arizona, where, along with playing for the Sting, he also did promotional work for the franchise, including visiting high schools and helping set up lacrosse programs in the Phoenix area. "I got a work-visa to play lacrosse, but I couldn't get a work-visa to do anything else," he says. After his rookie season, he got a pay increase that more than doubled his salary, and decided to commute to games via plane and move back to Victoria to pursue his other dream—becoming a full-time firefighter.

However, by the way McKay describes the selection process for being a firefighter, it may be easier to play professional lacrosse.

"Fire departments only have try-outs once every year, or once every two years," he says. "First, you have to meet all of the basic requirements: no criminal record, a clean driving record, completion of a fire training program and CPR. Then, there's the physical fitness test, then the aptitude test, then the interview. Finally, they select ten to fifteen people, but that still doesn't mean you get the job. There are a limited number of slots. You have to wait for someone to retire."

"I tried out two years ago for the Victoria Fire Department," he says. "I made it through a couple of cuts, but didn't get to the finals. I am trying again for a different fire department, the Saanich Fire Department, a small municipality within Victoria."

Now, while playing for the Sting and waiting to hear that "fire siren," McKay works as an assistant coach at Victoria's Claremont High School, and also at Pacific Sports Agency, a company that arranges lacrosse camps to develop high school talent.

"I act as a talent scout, advisor, regional coach and strength and conditioning trainer," he says. "We have identified some talented kids that may one day play in the NLL. I like to joke with kids that they are going to be the ones who make money in the NLL. And I enjoy being one of the pioneers who's helping the league grow."

Pat Jones

DEFENDING THE COUNTRY,
DEFENDING THE GOAL

At a nuclear facility in Pickering, Ontario, one of the employees identified what potentially could have been a pipe-bomb and notified the police detail that was guarding the facility. One of the guards was Pat Jones.

"Ever since I was a kid I wanted to be a police officer," Jones says. "On our special detail, we have procedures that include evacuating the plant quickly and calling the bomb squad. In this instance, the threat turned out to be a fake. Unfortunately, there are lots of materials that can look like a pipe bomb."

After the attacks in the U.S. on September 11, 2001, the Canadian government passed laws mandating that certain high-risk facilities, such as nuclear power plants, have increased security. Jones works close to fifty hours a week, often working alongside fellow pro lacrosse player and former teammate Dan Ladouceur.

What Jones does on a day-to-day basis when not carrying a lacrosse stick is classified.

"We cannot comment on his work," says his supervisor, Sergeant Wally Wilson. "In order to perform these jobs, Pat and

Dan and the other members of the special had to go through a background check and obtain a Level-2 security clearance. I can tell you the team members are well trained in firearms and self-defense, and we do physical training every day. But I cannot tell you anything beyond that. We are not even allowed to tell our wives the specific things we do on a daily basis."

Wilson could say, however, that Jones is in the best physical shape of anyone in his unit. "Other than his work-out regime, I would never know he was a professional lacrosse player," says Wilson, who describes Jones as "a laid-back guy, easy-going, easy-to-work-with, and respectful of his colleagues."

Canada's civil defense is in good hands with Jones—and so are the Portland Lumberjax of the National Lacrosse League where Jones, when not defending Canada from nuclear terrorism, serves as a defenseman.

Jones's professional lacrosse career nearly ended before it started.

Jones, who grew up in Oshawa, Ontario, played lacrosse as a kid, and later had an outstanding career playing in the Junior A league lacrosse for Whitby, Ontario. In 1998, he was drafted by the Hamilton Raiders (now the Toronto Rock) and eagerly reported to camp.

"We were practicing some defensive drills," he says. "Someone would set a pick on you, and you were supposed to fight around it and stay with your man. As I was going around, my foot got stuck in the Astroturf. I heard this pop and I crumpled to the ground. That was six knee surgeries ago."

Jones had torn his anterior cruciate ligament (ACL) that crisscrosses the knee. He was unable to play in a single game for the Raiders. So instead, he focused on his non-athletic career, and enrolled at the University of Western Ontario.

"It was a depressing time for me," Jones says of the years between 1998 until his return to the sport in 2003. "I would start to comeback, injure my knee again, and require more surgery. It usually happened when I rushed into a corner for a loose ball, and slammed on the brakes. Finally, I just concentrated on school and tried to get healthy."

During his rehabilitation period, Jones completed his police studies, and was fortunate: he was not too injured to pass the police physical.

"The physical featured some running tests, running with a weight vest, balance tests, climbing a six-foot wall, and lifting," he says. "I was lucky. I had recovered enough to pass without a problem."

And so began Pat Jones' police career, mostly as a beat cop working four days on and four days off, investigating thefts, robberies, domestic problems and vehicle accidents.

"Sometimes I felt like a laughing stock because I hadn't appeared in one NLL game, but I knew I could play," he says, "Although, in terms of my police career, it was the best thing that could have happened to me. However, once I was finally healthy, I couldn't wait to prove myself on the lacrosse field."

And so, after several years of rehabilitation, Jones gave his professional lacrosse dream one last shot. The Hamilton Raiders by now had become the Toronto Rock. Jones used his lacrosse connections to get a try-out.

"I chose that team because of geography," he says. "It was close to my work."

He did make the team, but he did not suit up for every game. In 2003, he played eleven games for the Rock; in 2004, only four. The inevitable phone call came. Jones had been traded to Anaheim.

"Some people felt bad for me, because here I was playing in front of 18,000 fans in Toronto's arena close to where my friends and family are, on one of the best teams in the NLL, then suddenly, I am traded to one of the worst teams. Anaheim was coming off a 1–15 season, the team played to only 4,000–5,000 fans, and I had to spend a lot of time on airplanes to get there."

In reality, the move gave Jones a great opportunity. In Anaheim, he was a regular player and appeared in all sixteen games played by the franchise in 2005. During that time, he also scored his first career professional goal.

"Toronto was so loaded with talent"—the Rock would go on to win the championship in 2005—"I couldn't get much playing time. In Anaheim, not only did I get to play, I was named one of the team captains. I gained experience and confidence."

He also gained valuable contacts. It was while playing for Anaheim that he met Angela Batinovich, who was to become the owner/president of the Portland Lumberjax franchise, and Jones's boss—after he ended up in Portland, after he was traded around the league like a Pokeman card.

When the Anaheim team folded at the end of the 2005 season, Jones was picked up by the Philadelphia Wings in the first round of the dispersal draft. The Wings promptly traded him to Minnesota. Minnesota then dealt him to Portland.

And there, he became the captain.

"He is everything you want as captain of a professional team," says Batinovich. "He commands respect. He keeps people in line. He is a born leader."

"He is down-to-earth, a solid player, and gives you everything he's got," says former Anaheim teammate and current Portland teammate Richard Morgan. "Pat is an all-around great guy."

Another fellow Lumberjax, winemaker Del Halladay says, "Pat is a quiet guy who is a little hard to get to know. He plays hard, and he leads by example. I can tell you, he has gained a lot of respect from the rest of the players on the team."

Just what you would expect from a guy who defuses bombs.

Index

OTHER TITLES FROM NEW CHAPTER PRESS

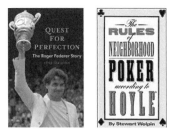 New Chapter Press is the publisher of *Weekend Warriors* and several other interesting titles, including *Quest for Perfection: The Roger Federer Story*, the first biography of the person many call the greatest tennis player of all time, as well as *The Rules of Neighborhood Poker according to Hoyle*. For more information, go to www.newchapterpressonline.com

FOR MORE INFORMATION

To follow up and learn more about some of the subjects in this book, we suggest you visit the following websites

National Lacrosse League – www.nll.com

US Lacrosse – www.uslacrosse.org

Major League Lacrosse – www.majorleaguelacrosse.com

Trilogy Lacrosse – www.trilogylacrosse.com

Maverik Lacrosse – www.maveriklacrosse.com

Elephant Island Wine – www.elephantislandwine.com